WORKING PAPERS FOR EXERCISES AND PROI
VOLUME 2: CHAPTERS 14–28 AND APPENDIXES A–D

FINANCIAL & MANAGERIAL ACCOUNTING

Fifth Edition

MANAGERIAL ACCOUNTING

Fifth Edition

WORKING PAPERS FOR EXERCISES AND PROBLEMS
VOLUME 2: CHAPTERS 14–28 AND APPENDIXES A–D

FINANCIAL & MANAGERIAL ACCOUNTING

Fifth Edition

MANAGERIAL ACCOUNTING

Fifth Edition

Belverd E. Needles, Jr.
DePaul University

Marian Powers
Northwestern University

Sherry K. Mills
New Mexico State University

Henry R. Anderson
Professor Emeritus, University of Central Florida

Consulting Author
James C. Caldwell
Andersen Consulting

Contributing Editor
Susan V. Crosson
Santa Fe Community College, Florida

Contributing Editor, Working Papers
Marion Taube
University of Pittsburgh

HOUGHTON MIFFLIN COMPANY BOSTON NEW YORK

Sponsoring Editor: Anne Kelly
Associate Sponsoring Editor: Margaret E. Monahan
Senior Manufacturing Coordinator: Priscilla Abreu

Printed in the U.S.A.

ISBN: 0-395-93573-3

123456789-WC-03 02 01 00 99

NOTE TO STUDENTS

This book contains Working Papers to be used in preparing solutions to all Exercises and Problems in Chapters 14–28 and Appendices of *Financial & Managerial Accounting,* Fifth Edition and Chapters 1–14 and Appendix A of *Managerial Accounting* , Fifth Edition. The Working Papers are designed to simplify your work; appropriate forms for computational assignments for each exercise and problem are provided, and some preliminary information has been printed to help you get started. Items requiring extensive written responses should be word processed or submitted on lined paper.

If you are using *Managerial Accounting,* Fifth Edition, the chapters of the textbook correspond to the Working Papers in this book in the following manner:

Managerial Chapter	**Working Papers** Chapter
1	15
2	16
3	17
4	18
5	19
6	20
7	21
8	22
9	23
10	24
11	25
12	26
13	14
14	27
Appendix A	Appendix D

Accounting Format Guide

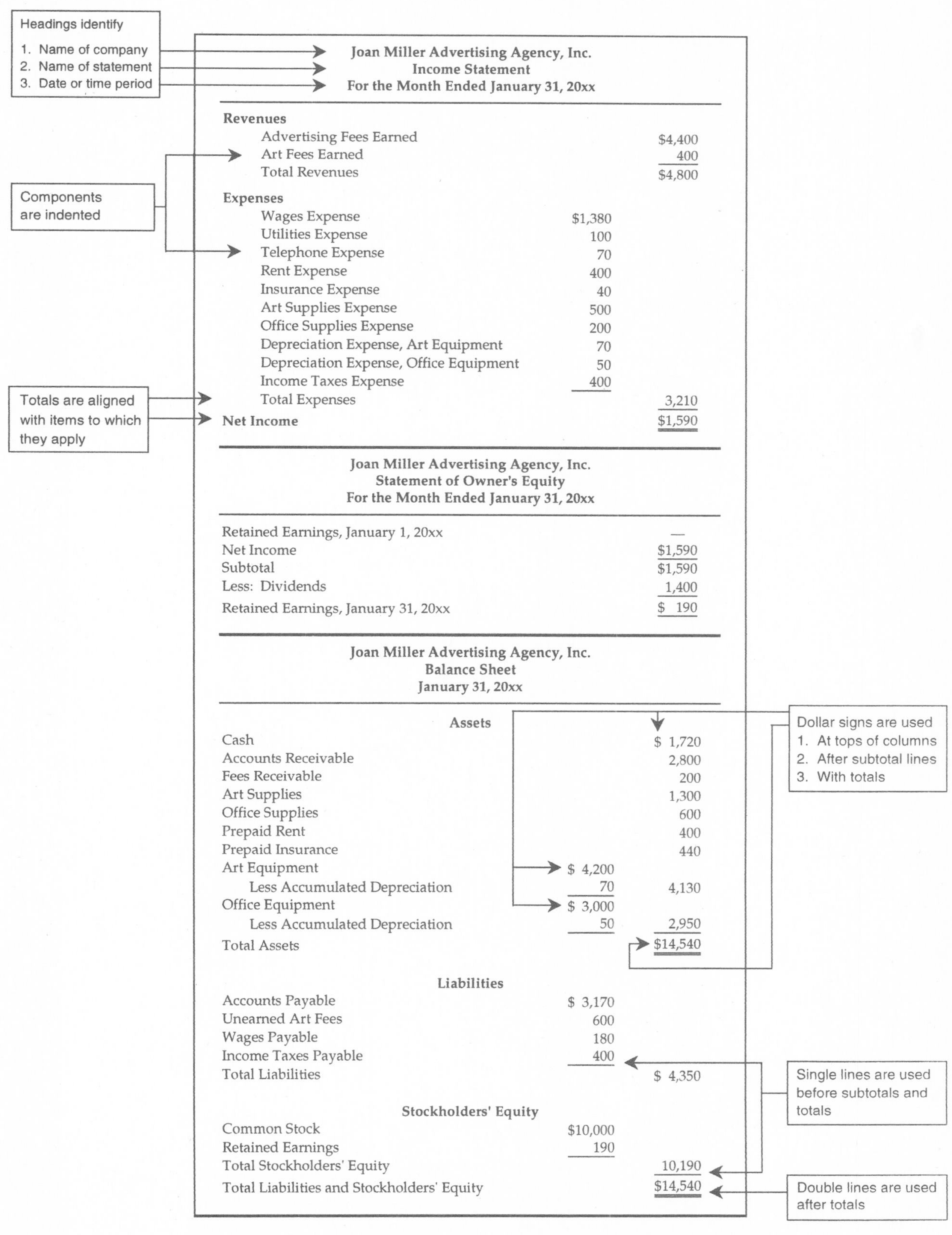

Joan Miller Advertising Agency, Inc.
Income Statement
For the Month Ended January 31, 20xx

Revenues		
Advertising Fees Earned		$4,400
Art Fees Earned		400
Total Revenues		$4,800
Expenses		
Wages Expense	$1,380	
Utilities Expense	100	
Telephone Expense	70	
Rent Expense	400	
Insurance Expense	40	
Art Supplies Expense	500	
Office Supplies Expense	200	
Depreciation Expense, Art Equipment	70	
Depreciation Expense, Office Equipment	50	
Income Taxes Expense	400	
Total Expenses		3,210
Net Income		$1,590

Joan Miller Advertising Agency, Inc.
Statement of Owner's Equity
For the Month Ended January 31, 20xx

Retained Earnings, January 1, 20xx	—
Net Income	$1,590
Subtotal	$1,590
Less: Dividends	1,400
Retained Earnings, January 31, 20xx	$ 190

Joan Miller Advertising Agency, Inc.
Balance Sheet
January 31, 20xx

Assets		
Cash		$ 1,720
Accounts Receivable		2,800
Fees Receivable		200
Art Supplies		1,300
Office Supplies		600
Prepaid Rent		400
Prepaid Insurance		440
Art Equipment	$ 4,200	
Less Accumulated Depreciation	70	4,130
Office Equipment	$ 3,000	
Less Accumulated Depreciation	50	2,950
Total Assets		$14,540
Liabilities		
Accounts Payable	$ 3,170	
Unearned Art Fees	600	
Wages Payable	180	
Income Taxes Payable	400	
Total Liabilities		$ 4,350
Stockholders' Equity		
Common Stock	$10,000	
Retained Earnings	190	
Total Stockholders' Equity		10,190
Total Liabilities and Stockholders' Equity		$14,540

WORKING PAPERS FOR EXERCISES AND PROBLEMS

VOLUME 2: CHAPTERS 14–28 AND APPENDIXES A–D

FINANCIAL & MANAGERIAL ACCOUNTING

Fifth Edition

MANAGERIAL ACCOUNTING

Fifth Edition

Name ______________________

Chapter 14, SE 1. Classification of Cash Flow Transactions

1.	4.
2.	5.
3.	6.

Chapter 14, SE 2. Cash-Generating Efficiency Ratios and Free Cash Flows

Cash Flow Yield	=	
	=	
Cash Flows to Sales	=	
	=	
Cash Flows to Assets	=	
	=	
Free Cash Flow	=	
	=	

Name

Chapter 14, SE 3. Cash Flow Efficiency and Free Cash Flow

Chapter 14, SE 4. Computing Cash Flows from Operating Activities: Indirect Method

Specialty Products Corporation
Schedule of Cash Flows from Operating Activities
For the Year Ended December 31, 20x1

Chapter 14, SE 5. Computing Cash Flows from Operating Activities: Indirect Method

Ayzarian Corporation
Schedule of Cash Flows from Operating Activities
For the Year Ended December 31, 20x1

Chapter 14, SE 6. Cash Flows from Investing Activities and Noncash Transactions

Chapter 14, SE 7. Cash Flows from Financing Activities

Name

Chapter 14, SE 8. Identifying Components of the Statement of Cash Flows

1.	5.
2.	6.
3.	7.
4.	8.

Chapter 14, SE 9. Cash Receipts from Sales and Cash Payments for Purchases: Direct Method

Cash Receipts from Sales	=
Cash Payments for Purchases	=

Chapter 14, SE 10. Cash Payments for Operating Expenses and Income Taxes: Direct Method

Cash Payments for Operating Expenses	=
Cash Payments for Income Taxes	=

Name

Chapter 14, E 1. Classification of Cash Flow Transactions

1.	6.	11.
2.	7.	12.
3.	8.	13.
4.	9.	
5.	10.	

Chapter 14, E 2. Cash-Generating Efficiency Ratios and Free Cash Flow

Cash Flow Yield	=	
	=	
Cash Flows to Sales	=	
	=	
Cash Flows to Assets	=	
	=	
Free Cash Flow	=	
	=	
	=	

Name

Chapter 14, E 3. Cash Flows from Operating Activities: Indirect Method

Union Chemical Company
Schedule of Cash Flows from Operating Activities
For the Year Ended December 31, 20x2

Chapter 14, E 4. Computing Cash Flows from Operating Activities: Indirect Method

Chapter 14, E 5. Preparing a Schedule of Cash Flows from Operating Activities: Indirect Method

Dedam Corporation
Schedule of Cash Flows from Operating Activities
For the Year Ended June 30, 20xx

Chapter 14, E 6. Computing Cash Flows from Investing Activities: Investments

Name

Chapter 14, E 7. Computing Cash Flows from Investing Activities: Plant Assets

Chapter 14, E 8. Determining Cash Flows from Investing and Financing Activities

Name

Chapter 14, E 9. Preparing the Statement of Cash Flows: Indirect Method

Bradbury Corporation
Statement of Cash Flows
For the Year Ended June 30, 20x2

Name ______________________

Chapter 14, E 10. Preparing a Work Sheet for the Statement of Cash Flows: Indirect Method

Bradbury Corporation
Work Sheet for Statement of Cash Flows
For the Year Ended June 30, 20x2

Description	Account Balances 20x1	Analysis of Transactions		Account Balances 20x2
		Debit	Credit	

Name

Chapter 14, E 11. Computing Cash Flows from Operating Activities: Direct Method

a.	Cash Receipts	=	Cash	+	Credit	+	Decrease in
	from Sales		Sales		Sales		Accounts Receivable
b.	Cash Payments	=					
	for Purchases						
c.	Cash Payments	=					
	for Operating						
	Expenses						
d.	Cash Payments	=					
	for Income Taxes						

Name

Chapter 14, E 12. Preparing a Schedule of Cash Flows from Operating Activities: Direct Method

Karsko Corporation
Schedule of Cash Flows from Operating Activities
For the Year Ended June 30, 20xx

a.	Cash Receipts	=	
	from Sales	=	
		=	
b.	Cash Payments	=	
	for Purchases		
		=	
		=	
c.	Cash Payments	=	
	for Operating		
	Expenses		
		=	
		=	
d.	Cash Payments	=	
	for Income Taxes		
		=	
		=	

Name ______________________

Chapter 14, P 1. Classification of Transactions

		Cash Flow Classification				Effect on Cash		
		Operating	Investing	Financing	Noncash			
	Transaction	Activity	Activity	Activity	Transaction	Increase	Decrease	No Effect
1.	Earned a net income.							
2.	Declared and paid cash dividend.							
3.	Issued stock for cash.							
4.	Retired long-term debt by issuing stock.							
5.	Paid accounts payable.							
6.	Purchased inventory with cash.							
7.	Purchased a one-year insurance policy with cash.							
8.	Purchased a long-term investment with cash.							
9.	Sold trading securities at a gain.							
10.	Sold a machine at a loss.							
11.	Retired fully depreciated equipment.							
12.	Paid interest on debt.							
13.	Purchased available-for-sale securities (long-term).							
14.	Received dividend income.							
15.	Received cash on account.							
16.	Converted bonds to common stock.							
17.	Purchased ninety-day Treasury bill.							

Name

Chapter 14, P 2. The Statement of Cash Flows: Indirect Method

1. Statement of cash flows prepared

Mateo Fabrics, Inc.
Statement of Cash Flows
For the Year Ended December 31, 20x3

Schedule of Noncash Investing and Financing Transactions

Name

2. Causes of increase in cash identified

3. Computation and assessment of cash flow yield and free cash flow

Name

Chapter 14, P 3. Statement of Cash Flows: Indirect Method

1. Statement of cash flows prepared

Bausch Ceramics, Inc.
Statement of Cash Flows
For the Year Ended December 31, 20x3

Schedule of Noncash Investing and Financing Transactions

2.	Causes of decrease in cash identified

3.	Computation and assessment of cash flow yield and free cash flow

Name

Chapter 14, P 4. The Work Sheet and the Statement of Cash Flows: Indirect Method

1. Work sheet prepared

Bausch Ceramics, Inc.
Work Sheet for Statement of Cash Flows
For the Year Ended December 31, 20x3

Description	Account Balances 12/31/x2	Analysis of Transactions Debit	Analysis of Transactions Credit	Account Balances 12/31/x3
Debits				
Credits				

Name

Description	Account Balances 12/31/x2	Analysis of Transactions: Debit	Analysis of Transactions: Credit	Account Balances 12/31/x3
Cash Flows from				
Operating Activities				
Cash Flows from				
Investing Activities				
Cash Flows from				
Financing Activities				

2. Same as solutions to required 1, 2, and 3 in P 3.

Name

Chapter 14, P 5. Cash Flows from Operating Activities: Direct Method

Broadwell Clothing Store
Schedule of Cash Flows from Operating Activities
For the Year Ended June 30, 20xx

a.	Cash Receipts	=	
	from Sales		
b.	Cash Payments	=	
	for Purchases		
c.	Cash Payments	=	
	for Operating		
	Expenses		
d.	Cash Payments	=	
	for Income Taxes		

Name

Chapter 14, P 6. Statement of Cash Flows: Direct Method

1. Statement of cash flows prepared

Gutierrez Corporation
Statement of Cash Flows
For the Year Ended June 30, 20x2

Schedule of Noncash Investing and Financing Transactions

1 (continued)

a.	**Cash Receipts**	=	
	from Sales		
b.	**Cash Payments**	=	
	for Purchases		
c.	**Cash Payments**	=	
	for Operating		
	Expenses		
d.	**Cash Payments**	=	
	for Income Taxes		

Name

1 (concluded)

	General Journal			
	Description	Post. Ref.	Debit	Credit
e.				

Name

2. Causes of increase in cash identified

3. Computation and assessment of cash flow yield and free cash flow

Cash Flow Yield	=	
	=	
Free Cash Flow	=	
	=	
	=	

Name ____________________

Chapter 14, P 7. Classification of Transactions

		Cash Flow Classification				Effect on Cash		
	Transaction	Operating Activity	Investing Activity	Financing Activity	Noncash Transaction	Increase	Decrease	No Effect
1.	Incurred a net loss.							
2.	Declared and issued a stock dividend.							
3.	Paid a cash dividend.							
4.	Collected accounts receivable.							
5.	Purchased inventory with cash.							
6.	Retired long-term debt with cash.							
7.	Sold available-for-sale securities at a loss.							
8.	Issued stock for equipment.							
9.	Purchased a one-year insurance policy with cash.							
10.	Purchased treasury stock with cash.							
11.	Retired a fully depreciated truck (no gain or loss).							
12.	Paid interest on note.							
13.	Received cash dividend on investment.							
14.	Sold treasury stock.							
15.	Paid income taxes.							
16.	Transferred cash to money market account.							
17.	Purchased land and building with a mortgage.							

Name

Chapter 14, P 8. The Statement of Cash Flows: Indirect Method

1. Statement of cash flows prepared

Meridian Corporation
Statement of Cash Flows
For the Year Ended December 31, 20x2

Schedule of Noncash Investing and Financing Transactions

Name

2. Causes of increase in cash identified

3. Computation and assessment of cash flow yield and free cash flow

Cash Flow Yield	=	
20x2:	=	
Free Cash Flow	=	
20x2:	=	

Name

Chapter 14, P 9. The Work Sheet and the Statement of Cash Flows: Indirect Method

1. Work sheet prepared

Meridian Corporation
Work Sheet for Statement of Cash Flows
For the Year Ended December 31, 20x2

Description	Account Balances 12/31/x1	Analysis of Transactions Debit	Analysis of Transactions Credit	Account Balances 12/31/x2

1 (Continued)

Description	Account Balances 12/31/x2	Analysis of Transactions		Account Balances 12/31/x3
		Debit	Credit	
Cash Flows from				
Operating Activities				
Cash Flows from				
Investing Activities				
Cash Flows from				
Financing Activities				

2. **Same as solutions to required 1, 2, and 3 in P 8.**

Name

Chapter 15, SE 1. Management Accounting Versus Financial Accounting

1.	4.	7.
2.	5.	8.
3.	6.	

Chapter 15, SE 2. The Management Cycle

1.	3.	5.
2.	4.	6.

Chapter 15, SE 3. JIT and Continuous Improvement

Form is not provided; student should use his/her own paper.

Chapter 15, SE 4. Analysis of Nonfinancial Data

Form is not provided; student should use his/her own paper.

Chapter 15, SE 5. Managerial Report Preparation

Form is not provided; student should use his/her own paper.

Chapter 15, SE 6. Merchandising Versus Manufacturing

Form is not provided; student should use his/her own paper.

Chapter 15, SE 7. Cost Classification

1.
2.
3.

Chapter 15, SE 8. Ethical Conduct

Form is not provided; student should use his/her own paper.

Name

Chapter 15, E 1. Definitions of Management Accounting

Chapter 15, E 2. The Management Cycle

1.	6.
2.	7.
3.	8.
4.	9.
5.	10.

Chapter 15, E 3. New Management Philosophies

Name ______________________

Chapter 15, E 4. Nonfinancial Data Analysis

	Thompson	May	Pratt	Yu	Hardin	Harty
Hours worked						
Square yards of sod planted						
Square yards that should have been planted (500 yd/person/hr x hr worked)						
Yards under (over) target						
Percent under (over) target						

Results of the analysis:

Chapter 15, E 5. Report Preparation

Form is not provided; student should use his/her own paper.

Chapter 15, E 6. Merchandising Versus Manufacturing

1.	6.
2.	7.
3.	8.
4.	9.
5.	

Chapter 15, E 7. Cost Classifications

		Cost Classification		
		Product or Period	Direct or Indirect	Variable or Fixed
Example: Bicycle tire		Product	Direct	Variable
1.	Depreciation on office computer			
2.	Labor to assemble bicycle			
3.	Labor to inspect bicycle			
4.	President's salary			
5.	Lubricant for wheels			

Chapter 15, E 8. Professional Ethics

Name

Chapter 15, P 1. Using Nonfinancial Data

1. **Analysis comparing maximum and actual numbers of rejected candy canes prepared**

Week 3, 20xx	Maximum Number of Rejected Candy Canes Allowed	Actual Number of Rejected Candy Canes	Variance Under (Over) Allowed Maximum
Monday			
Tuesday			
Wednesday			
Thursday			
Friday			
Total for the Week			
Daily Average			

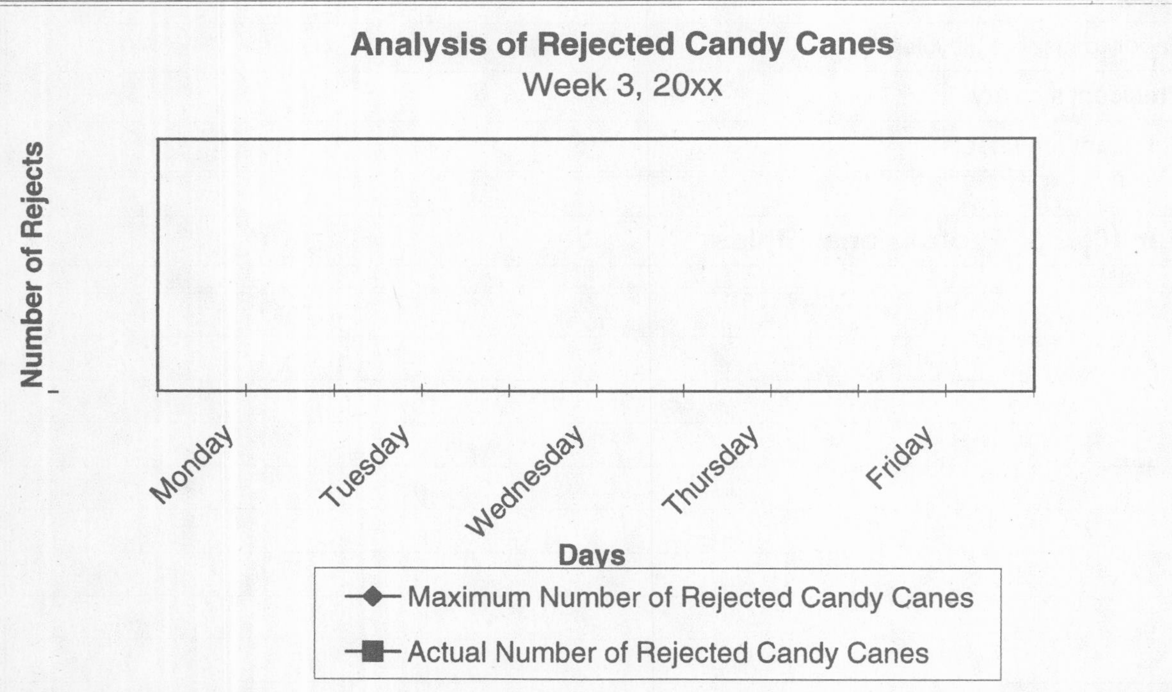

2. Analysis comparing number of rejects for each category for Week 1 and Week 3 prepared

	Reasons for Rejects Week 1, 20xx	Reasons for Rejects Week 3, 20xx	Decrease (Increase) in Number of Rejects
Ingredients			
Shaping			
Cooking Time			
Total			

Comparison of Reasons

3. Success in increasing the quality of candy discussed

Form is not provided; student should use his/her own paper.

Name

Chapter 15, P 2. Nonfinancial Data Analysis: Manufacturing

1. Analyses showing average actual hours worked per pair of shoes produced

Hours worked per pair of shoes	=	actual hours worked each day
		÷ number of pairs of shoes produced each day

Department	Monday (1,200 pairs)	Tuesday (1,240 pairs)	Wednesday (1,220 pairs)	Thursday (1,250 pairs)	Friday (1,230 pairs)
Cutting/Lining (hr/pair)					
Molding (hr/pair)					
Bonding (hr/pair)					
Soling (hr/pair)					
Finishing (hr/pair)					

Name ______________________

2. Analyses comparing estimated hours to average actual hours per pair of shoes produced

Cutting/Lining	**Monday**	**Tuesday**	**Wednesday**	**Thursday**	**Friday**
Actual hr/pair					
Est. hr/pair					
Hours under (over)					
Percent under (over) target					
Molding	**Monday**	**Tuesday**	**Wednesday**	**Thursday**	**Friday**
Actual hr/pair					
Est. hr/pair					
Hours under (over)					
Percent under (over) target					
Bonding	**Monday**	**Tuesday**	**Wednesday**	**Thursday**	**Friday**
Actual hr/pair					
Est. hr/pair					
Hours under (over)					
Percent under (over) target					
Soling	**Monday**	**Tuesday**	**Wednesday**	**Thursday**	**Friday**
Actual hr/pair					
Est. hr/pair					
Hours under (over)					
Percent under (over) target					
Finishing	**Monday**	**Tuesday**	**Wednesday**	**Thursday**	**Friday**
Actual hr/pair					
Est. hr/pair					
Hours under (over)					
Percent under (over) target					

Name ______________________

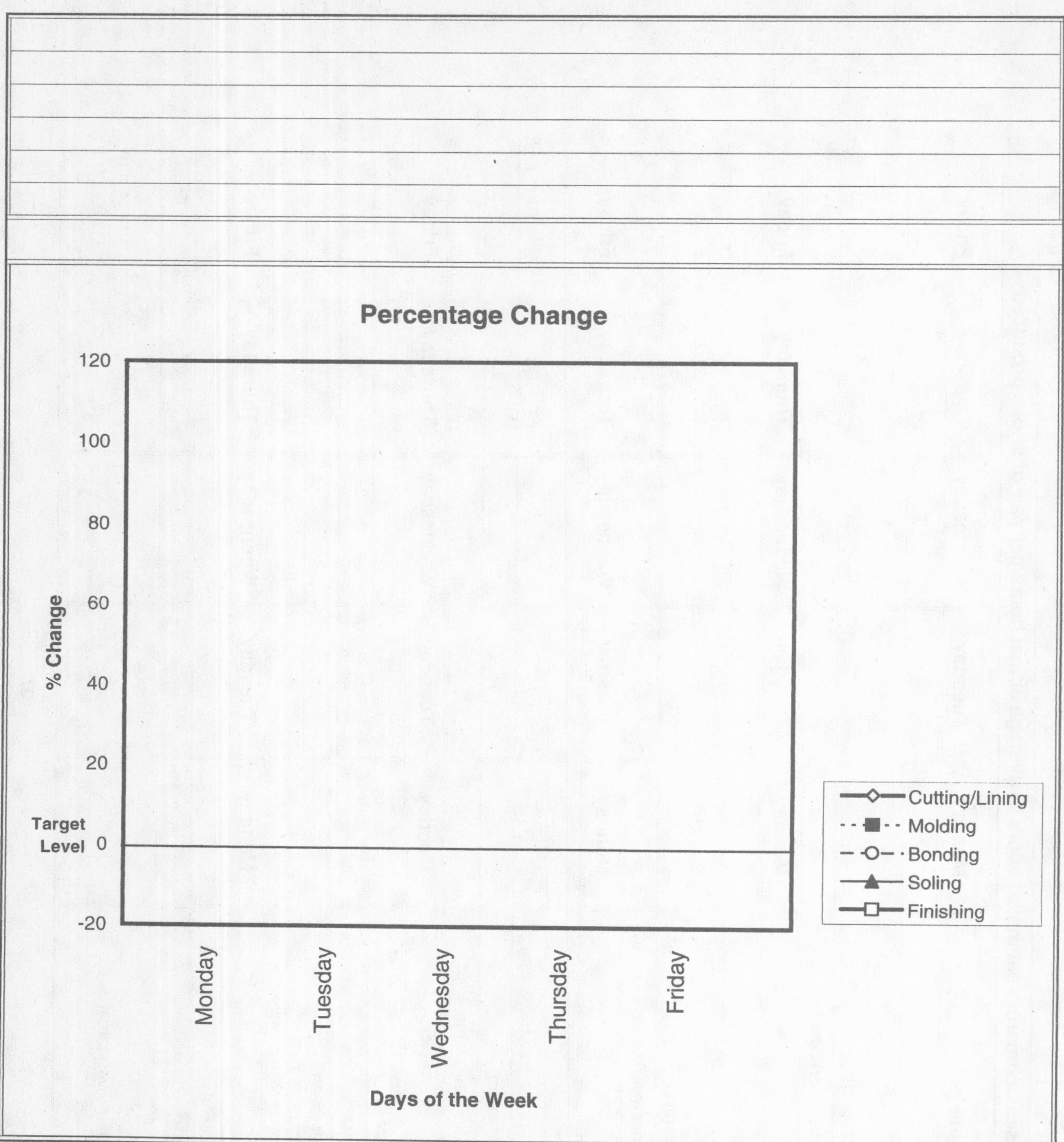
Percentage Change
120
100
80
60
40
20
Target Level 0
-20
% Change
Monday
Tuesday
Wednesday
Thursday
Friday
Days of the Week
Cutting/Lining
Molding
Bonding
Soling
Finishing

Name

Chapter 15, P 3. Approach to Report Preparation

Student should use his/her own paper to complete the problem.

Name ______________________

Chapter 15, P 4. Manufacturing Company Balance Sheet			
1.	**Accounts in manufacturing and merchandising organizations identified**		
2.	**Key figures calculated**		
a.	**Gross Margin**	=	+
		=	
		=	
b.	**Cost of Goods Sold**	=	−
		=	
		=	
c.	**Cost of Goods Available for Sale**	=	+
		=	
		=	
d.	**Cost of Goods Manufactured**	=	−
		=	
		=	

Name

Chapter 15, P 5. Inventories, Cost of Goods Sold, and Net Income

1. Missing data for a merchandising organization calculated

Note: Items are listed in the suggested order of solution.

First Quarter:							
a.	Gross Margin	=	Sales	–	Cost of Goods Sold		
		=				=	
c.	Operating Expenses	=	Gross Margin	–	Net Income		
		=				=	
d.	Cost of Goods Available for Sale	=	Cost of Goods Sold	+	Ending Merchandise Inventory		
		=				=	
b.	Net Cost of Purchases	=	Cost of Goods Available for Sale	–	Beginning Merchandise Inventory		
		=				=	
Second Quarter:							
e.	Sales	=	Gross Margin	+	Cost of Goods Sold		
		=				=	
f.	Ending Merchandise Inventory	=	Cost of Goods Available for Sale	–	Cost of Goods Sold		
		=				=	
g.	Beginning Merchandise Inventory	=	Cost of Goods Available for Sale	–	Net Cost of Purchases		
		=				=	

Name

Third Quarter:							
h.	Beginning Merchandise Inventory	=	Cost of Goods Available for Sale	–	Net Cost of Purchases		
		=				=	
i.	Net Income	=	Gross Margin	–	Operating Expenses		
		=				=	
j.	Cost of Goods Sold	=	Sales	–	Gross Margin		
		=				=	
Fourth Quarter:							
l.	Gross Margin	=	Operating Expenses	+	Net Income		
		=				=	
k.	Sales	=	Gross Margin	+	Cost of Goods Sold		
		=				=	
m.	Ending Merchandise Inventory	=	Cost of Goods Available for Sale	–	Cost of Goods Sold		
		=				=	
n.	Net Cost of Purchases	=	Cost of Goods Available for Sale	–	Beginning Merchandise Inventory		
		=				=	

Name

2.	Missing data for a manufacturing organization calculated					
First Quarter:						
c.	Sales	=	Gross Margin	+	Cost of Goods Sold	
		=				=
a.	Ending Finished Goods Inventory	=	Cost of Goods Available for Sale	−	Cost of Goods Sold	
		=				=
b.	Beginning Finished Goods Inventory	=	Cost of Goods Available for Sale	−	Cost of Goods Manufactured	
		=				=
Second Quarter:						
f.	Gross Margin	=	Sales	−	Cost of Goods Sold	
		=				=
g.	Operating Expenses	=	Gross Margin	−	Net Income	
		=				=
d.	Cost of Goods Available for Sale	=	Cost of Goods Sold	+	Ending Finished Goods Inventory	
		=				=
e.	Cost of Goods Manufactured	=	Cost of Goods Available for Sale	−	Beginning Finished Goods Inventory	
		=				=

Name ____________________

Third Quarter:							
j.	Gross Margin	=	Operating Expenses	+	Net Income		
		=				=	
k.	Sales	=	Gross Margin	+	Cost of Goods Sold		
		=				=	
h.	Ending Finished Goods Inventory	=	Cost of Goods Available for Sale	–	Cost of Goods Sold		
		=				=	
i.	Cost of Goods Manufactured	=	Cost of Goods Available for Sale	–	Beginning Finished Goods Inventory		
		=				=	
Fourth Quarter:							
n.	Beginning Finished Goods Inventory	=	Cost of Goods Available for Sale	–	Cost of Goods Manufactured		
		=				=	
m.	Net Income	=	Gross Margin	–	Operating Expenses		
		=				=	
l.	Cost of Goods Sold	=	Sales	–	Gross Margin		
		=				=	

Name ____________________

Chapter 15, P 6. Nonfinancial Data Analysis: Manufacturing

1. Analyses showing average actual labor hours worked per board prepared

Hours worked per board = hours worked each week ÷ boards produced each week

	WEEK 1		WEEK 2		WEEK 3		WEEK 4	
	First Shift	Second Shift	First Shift	Second Shift	First Shift	Second Shift	First Shift	Second Shift
Department	(120 boards)	(100 boards)	(135 boards)	(105 boards)	(140 boards)	(115 boards)	(130 boards)	(110 boards)
Molding (hr/board)								
Sanding (hr/board)								
Fiber-Ap (hr/board)								
Finishing (hr/board)								

2. Analyses comparing estimated hours per board to actual hours per board prepared

	WEEK 1		WEEK 2		WEEK 3		WEEK 4	
	First Shift	Second Shift	First Shift	Second Shift	First Shift	Second Shift	First Shift	Second Shift
MOLDING	(120 boards)	(100 boards)	(135 boards)	(105 boards)	(140 boards)	(115 boards)	(130 boards)	(110 boards)
Actual hr/board								
Est. hr/board								
Hours under								
(over) target								
Percent under								
(over) target								
	WEEK 1		WEEK 2		WEEK 3		WEEK 4	
	First Shift	Second Shift	First Shift	Second Shift	First Shift	Second Shift	First Shift	Second Shift
SANDING	(120 boards)	(100 boards)	(135 boards)	(105 boards)	(140 boards)	(115 boards)	(130 boards)	(110 boards)
Actual hr/board								
Est. hr/board								
Hours under								
(over) target								
Percent under								
(over) target								

Name ____________

2 (continued)

	WEEK 1		WEEK 2		WEEK 3		WEEK 4	
	First Shift	Second Shift	First Shift	Second Shift	First Shift	Second Shift	First Shift	Second Shift
FIBER-AP	(120 boards)	(100 boards)	(135 boards)	(105 boards)	(140 boards)	(115 boards)	(130 boards)	(110 boards)
Actual hr/board								
Est. hr/board								
Hours under (over) target								
Percent under (over) target								

	WEEK 1		WEEK 2		WEEK 3		WEEK 4	
	First Shift	Second Shift	First Shift	Second Shift	First Shift	Second Shift	First Shift	Second Shift
FINISHING	(120 boards)	(100 boards)	(135 boards)	(105 boards)	(140 boards)	(115 boards)	(130 boards)	(110 boards)
Actual hr/board								
Est. hr/board								
Hours under (over) target								
Percent under (over) target								

Name

Chapter 15, P 7. Approach to Report Preparation

Student should use his/her own paper to complete the problem.

Name ______________________

Chapter 15, P 8. Manufacturing Organization Balance Sheet

1. Accounts in manufacturing and merchandising organizations identified

2. Key figures calculated

a.	Gross Margin	=	
		=	
		=	
b.	Cost of Goods Sold	=	
		=	
		=	
c.	Cost of Goods Available for Sale	=	
		=	
		=	
d.	Cost of Goods Manufactured	=	
		=	
		=	

Name

Chapter 16, SE 1. Distinguishing the Costs of a Product

Chapter 16, SE 2. Elements of Manufacturing Cost

1.
2.
3.
4.
5.
6.
7.

Chapter 16, SE 3. Computing Product Unit Cost

Chapter 16, SE 4. Manufacturing Cost Flow

Direct Materials Inventory, ending balance:

Work in Process Inventory, ending balance:

Finished Goods Inventory, ending balance:

Chapter 16, SE 5. Document Flows for a Manufacturing Organizaiton

1.
2.
3.
4.
5.
6.
7.

Chapter 16, SE 6. Income Statement for a Manufacturing Organization

C.L.I.N.T. Company
Income Statement
For the Year Ended December 31, 20xx

Chapter 16, SE 7. Calculation of Underapplied or Overapplied Overhead

Applied manufacturing overhead	
Less actual manufacturing overhead	
Overapplied	

Chapter 16, SE 8. Computation of Predetermined Overhead Rate

Predetermined Overhead Rate per Service Request	=	
	=	
	=	

Chapter 16, SE 9. Application of Manufacturing Overhead to Production

Manufacturing Overhead Costs Applied	=	

Chapter 16, SE 10. Activity-Based Costing and Cost Drivers

Cutting/Stitching activity

Trimming/Packing activity

Designing activity

Chapter 16, SE 11. Unit Costs in a Service Business

Name

Chapter 16, E 1. Distinguishing the Costs of Products

1.	6.
2.	7.
3.	8.
4.	9.
5.	10.

Chapter 16, E 2. Unit Cost Determination

1. Unit cost computed

Cost Items	Total Cost	Unit Cost (Total ÷ 10,550)
Direct Materials		
Olen Millot grapes	22155 —	
Chancellor grapes	9495 —	
Bottles	5275 —	
Total direct materials costs		
Direct Labor		
Pickers/loaders	2110 —	
Crusher	422 —	
Processors	8440 —	
Bottler	1688 —	
Storage and racking	11605 —	
Total direct labor costs		
Manufacturing overhead		
Depreciation, equipment	2743 —	
Depreciation, building	5275 —	
Utilities	1055 —	
Indirect labor	6330 —	
Supervision	7385 —	
Supplies	3165 —	
Storage fixtures	2532 —	
Chemicals	4220 —	
Repairs	1477 —	
Miscellaneous	633 —	
Total manufacturing overhead cost	34815 —	
Total production costs	96005 —	

Name

E 2 (concluded)

2.	Recommendation made

Chapter 16, E 3. Documentation

Memo

Name

Chapter 16, E 4. Cost Flows and Inventory Accounts

1.
2.
3.
4.
5.
6.
7.

Chapter 16, E 5. Statement of Cost of Goods Manufactured

Earth Company
Statement of Cost of Goods Manufactured
For the Month Ended August 31, 20xx

Name

Chapter 16, E 6. Computation of Predetermined Overhead Rate

1 and 2. **20x1 and 20x2 predetermined overhead rates computed**

	(1)	(2)	(3)
		20x2	20x2
	20x1	Percentage	(1 x 2)
Indirect materials and supplies			
Repairs and maintenance			
Outside service contracts			
Indirect labor			
Factory supervision			
Depreciation, machinery			
Factory insurance			
Property taxes			
Heat, light, and power			
Miscellaneous manufacturing overhead			
Totals			
Divided by machine hours			
Predetermined overhead rates			

Name

Chapter 16, E 7. Computation and Application of Overhead Rate

1. Anticipated manufacturing overhead determined

2. Manufacturing overhead rate computed

3. Manufacturing overhead applied

Chapter 16, E 8. Disposition of Overapplied Overhead

1. Overhead applied to operations computed

2. Overapplied overhead computed

3. Effect of overapplied overhead on Cost of Goods Sold determined

Name ______________________

Chapter 16, E 9. Activities and Activity-Based Costing

Traditional costing approach

Activity-based costing approach

Activities	Cost Pool Rates			Order HQ14 Activity Usage			
Income materials inspection	$17.50	per type of material	x	17	types of materials	=	
In-process inspection	$ 0.06	per product	x	2,400	products	=	
Tool and gauge control	$26.50	per process	x	11	processes	=	
Product certification	$94.00	per order	x	1	order	=	
Total quality control costs assigned to Order HQ14							

Chapter 16, E 10. Unit Costs in a Service Business

Total costs		
Cost per bale	=	
Revenue per bale	=	

Comment:

Name

Chapter 16, P 1. Computation of Unit Cost

1 and 2. **Unit cost by department and total unit cost computed**

Department 85:

Department 82:

3. **Analysis of the JAZ Company order**

Name

Chapter 16, P 2. Statement of Cost of Goods Manufactured

Name ____________________

Chapter 16, P 3. Statement of Cost of Goods Manufactured and Cost of Goods Sold

	Clovis Division	Lamesa Division	Childress Division	Grady Division
Direct materials used			(g)	
Direct labor costs	(a)			
Manufacturing overhead costs				(j)
Total manufacturing costs		(d)	(h)	
Beginning Work in Process Inventory		(e)		(l)
Ending Work in Process Inventory	(b)			
Cost of goods manufactured				(k)
Beginning Finished Goods Inventory		(f)		
Ending Finished Goods Inventory			(i)	
Cost of goods sold	(c)			

Name ____________________

Chapter 16, P 4. Application of Manufacturing Overhead

1. Predetermined overhead rate computed

Classic Cosmetics Company
Overhead Rate Computation Schedule
For the Year Ended December 31, 20x2

Overhead Cost Item	(1) 20xx	(2) 20x1	(3) Amount of Increase (2 – 1)	(4) Percentage Increase (2 ÷ 1)	(5) Projection 20x2 (2 x 4)
Indirect labor	18100 —	23530 —			
Employee benefits	22000 —	28600 —			
Manufacturing supervision	16800 —	18480 —			
Utilities	10350 —	14490 —			
Factory insurance	6500 —	7800 —			
Janitorial services	11000 —	12100 —			
Depreciation, factory and machinery	17750 —	21300 —			
Miscellaneous manufacturing overhead	5750 —	7475 —			
Total manufacturing overhead	108250 —	133775 —			

Predetermined overhead rate for 20x2:

Name

2. Amount of applied overhead determined

Job No.	Machine Hours	Predetermined Overhead Rate	Overhead Applied*
2214	12,300		
2215	14,200		
2216	9,800		
2217	13,600		
2218	11,300		
2219	8,100		

3. Computation and adjustment of underapplied or overapplied overhead

Name

Chapter 16, P 5. Activities and Activity-Based Costing

1 and 2.	Total costs assigned to the Holstrum order

	Traditional Costing Approach	Activity-Based Costing Approach

3.	Cost difference discussed

Form is not provided; student should use his/her own paper.

Name

Chapter 16, P 6. Application of Manufacturing Overhead

1. Predetermined overhead rate computed

Overhead Cost Item	(1) 20x1	(2) 20x2	(3) Amount of Increase (2 – 1)	(4) Percentage Increase (2 ÷ 1)	(5) Projection 20x3 (2 x 4)
Indirect materials	44500 —	57850 —			
Indirect labor	21200 —	25440 —			
Supervision	37800 —	41580 —			
Utilities	9400 —	11280 —			
Labor-related costs	8200 —	9020 —			
Depreciation, factory	9800 —	10780 —			
Depreciation, machinery	22700 —	27240 —			
Property taxes	2400 —	2880 —			
Insurance	1600 —	1920 —			
Miscellaneous manufacturing overhead	4400 —	4840 —			
Total manufacturing overhead	162000 —	192830 —			

Predetermined overhead rate for 20x3:

Name

2.	Amount of applied overhead determined

Job No.	Actual Machine Hours	x	Rate	Overhead Applied

3.	Computation and adjustment of underapplied or overapplied overhead

Chapter 16, P 7. Activities and Activity-Based Costing

1 and 2. **Total costs assigned to the Hines order**

	Traditional Costing Approach	Activity-Based Costing Approach

3. **Cost differences discussed**

Form is not provided; student should use his/her own paper.

Name

Chapter 16, P 8. Application of Manufacturing Overhead: Traditional and Activity-Based Costing Approaches

1. Calculations using activity-based costing

a. Overhead cost pool rates calculated

	Column 1	Column 2	Column 1 ÷ Column 2
	Estimated		
	Activity	Total Estimated	
Overhead Activity Pool	Cost Pool	Cost Driver Level	Cost Pool Rate

Name ______________________

1 (continued)

b. Overhead costs applied

Overhead Cost Pool	Cost Pool Rate	Rigger II Cost Driver Level	Rigger II Cost Applied	BioScout Cost Driver Level	BioScout Cost Applied
Setup	per setup	setups		setups	
Inspection	per inspection	inspections		inspections	
Engineering	per engineering hour	engineering hours		engineering hours	
Assembly	per machine hour	machine hours		machine hours	
Total overhead costs applied					
Number of units					
Overhead cost per unit					

c. Product unit cost calculated

Product costs per unit:	Rigger II	BioScout
Direct materials		
Direct labor		
Manufacturing overhead		
Product unit cost		

2. Differences in assigned costs discussed

Name

Chapter 17, SE 1. Uses of Product Costing Information

1.
2.
3.

Chapter 17, SE 2. Industries Using a Job Order Costing System

1.	4.
2.	5.
3.	

Chapter 17, SE 3. Job Order Versus Process Costing Systems

1.	4.
2.	5.
3.	6.

Chapter 17, SE 4. Manufacturing Transactions in a Job Order Costing System

1.
2.
3.
4.

Chapter 17, SE 5. Transactions in a Job Order Costing System

Work in Process Inventory Control

Service Overhead Control

Marketing Expense

Factory Labor

Chapter 17, SE 6. Cost of Product Costing

1.	4.
2.	5.
3.	6.

Chapter 17, SE 7. Computation of Product Unit Cost for a Project

Job Order		**Gatekeeper 3000**	
No. ______		**Apache City, North Dakota**	
Customer:		**Direct Materials:**	
Robert Arthur		Dept. 1	$ 3,540
		Dept. 2	2,820
Date of Order:		Total	$
April 4, 20xx			
		Direct Labor:	
Date of Completion:		Dept. 1	$ 2,340
June 18, 20xx		Dept. 2	1,620
		Total	$
Cost Summary			
Direct Materials	$	**Applied Manufacturing Overhead:**	
Direct Labor		Dept. 1	$ 2,880
Manufacturing Overhead		Dept. 2	2,550
Total	$	Total	$
Units Completed			
Product Unit Cost	$		

Chapter 17, SE 8. Job Order Costing in a Service Organization

1.
2.
3.
4.

Name

Chapter 17, E 1. Product Costing

1.	6.
2.	7.
3.	8.
4.	9.
5.	10.

Chapter 17, E 2. Costing Systems: Industry Linkage

a.	i.
b.	j.
c.	k.
d.	l.
e.	m.
f.	n.
g.	o.
h.	p.

Chapter 17, E 3. Job Order Cost Flow

Form is not provided; student should use his/her own paper.

Name ______________________

Chapter 17, E 4. Work in Process Inventory Control Account: T Account Analysis

1. T accounts prepared

Materials Inventory Control	

Work in Process Inventory Control	

Manufacturing Overhead Control	

Payroll Payable	

2. Ending balance computed

Work in Process Inventory Control account:	
Ending balance, July 31, 20xx	

Name ______________________

Chapter 17, E 5. Job Order Costs and Computation of Product Unit Cost

JOB ORDER COST CARD

Kasik Cabinet Company

Job Order No.

Product Specs:

Customer:		Direct Materials:	
		Cedar	$
		Pine	
		Hardware	
		Supplies	
Date of Order:		Total	$
		Direct Labor:	
Date of Completion:		Sawing	$
		Shaping	
		Finishing	
		Assembly	
		Total	$
Cost Summary		Applied Manufacturing Overhead:	
Direct Materials	$	Sawing (x)	$
Direct Labor		Shaping (x)	
Manufacturing Overhead		Finishing (x)	
		Assembly (x)	
Total	$	Total	$

Units Completed

Product Unit Cost: $ ÷ cabinets = $______ per cabinet

Name

Chapter 17, E 6. Computation of Product Unit Cost

Total manufacturing costs:	
Liability insurance, manufacturing	
Depreciation, manufacturing equipment	
Materials used	
Indirect labor, manufacturing	
Manufacturing supplies	
Heat, light, and power, manufacturing	
Fire insurance, manufacturing	
Rent, manufacturing	
Direct labor	
Manager's salary, manufacturing	
Total manufacturing costs	
Computation of product unit cost:	

Name

Chapter 17, E 7. Computation of Product Unit Cost

1. Total cost of each job computed

Wild Iris Corporation
Special Cost Analysis

	Job Order Cost Cards		
	Job A–25	Job A–27	Job B–14
Direct materials			
Fabric Q	10840 —	12980 —	17660 —
Fabric Z	11400 —	12200 —	13440 —
Fabric YB	5260 —	6920 —	10900 —
Totals			
Direct labor			
Garmentmaker	8900 —	10400 —	16200 —
Layout	6450 —	7425 —	9210 —
Packaging	3950 —	4875 —	6090 —
Totals			
Manufacturing Overhead			
120% of direct labor dollars			
Total cost			

2. Product unit cost of each job computed

	Job A–25	Job A–27	Job B–14
Units produced	700	775	1482
Product unit cost			

Chapter 17, E 8. Job Costing in a Service Organization

JOB ORDER COST CARD

Clovis Computer Services

Customer: Ray Dove
Job Order No:
Contract Type: Cost-Plus
Type of Service: Software Installation and Internet Interfacing
Date of Completion: October 6, 20xx

Costs Charged to Job	Total
Software Installation Services	
Installation labor	$300
Service overhead (50% of installation labor costs)	
Total	$450
Internet Services	
Internet labor	$200
Service overhead (20% of Internet labor costs)	40
Total	
COST SUMMARY TO DATE:	**Total Cost**
Software Installation Services	$
Internet Services	
Total	$
Profit margin	
Contract revenue	$

Name

Chapter 17, P 1. Job Order Costing: Unknown Quantity Analysis

	June	July
Materials Inventory Control:		
Beginning balance	(a)	(e)
Purchases		
Requisitions		(g)
Ending balance		
Work in Process Inventory Control:		
Beginning balance		(f)
Direct materials requisitioned		(g)
Direct labor costs		
Manufacturing overhead applied	(b)	(h)
Ending balance	(d)	(j)
Cost of units completed	(c)	
Finished Goods Inventory Control:		
Beginning balance		(g)
Transfers from Work in Process Inventory Control	(c)	
Transfers to Cost of Goods Sold		(i)
Ending balance		

Chapter 17, P 2. Job Order Costing: T Account Analysis

1. Entries recorded in T accounts

Materials Inventory Control

Work in Process Inventory Control

Finished Goods Inventory Control

Manufacturing Overhead Control

Job X

Factory Labor

Sales

Name

1 (continued)

Job Y

Cash

Job Z

Prepaid Insurance

Cost of Goods Sold

Accumulated Depreciation, Machinery

Accounts Payable

Selling and Administrative Expenses

Accounts Receivable

Property Taxes Payable

2. Underapplied overhead computed

Manufacturing overhead incurred	
Manufacturing overhead applied	
Underapplied overhead	

Manufacturing Overhead Control

Cost of Goods Sold

Chapter 17, P 3. Job Order Cost Flow

1. Transactions reconstructed using T accounts
4. Ending inventory balances computed

Materials Inventory Control

Finished Goods Inventory Control

Manufacturing Overhead Control

Work in Process Inventory Control

Payroll Payable

Cost of Goods Sold

Sales

Accounts Receivable

Ending Work in Process Inventory Control:

Job 24–A	$
Job 24–B	
Job 24–C	
Job 24–D	
Total	$

2. Cost of completed units computed

Cost of ending Work in Process Inventory Control:

Job No.	Direct Materials	Direct Labor	Manufacturing Overhead	Total
24–A				
24–B				
24–C				
24–D				

Costs of units completed:

Cost of goods completed and transferred	

3. Cost of units sold computed

Name

5. Product unit costs computed	
Job 24–A:	
Job 24–C:	

Chapter 17, P 4. Job Order Costing: Service Company

1. Job order cost cards created

JOB ORDER COST CARD
Nedeau Engineering Co.

Customer: Customer A
Job Order No.: P–12
Contract Type: Cost-Plus
Specs:
Date Completed: Jan. 31, 20xx

Costs Charged to Job	Previous Months	Current Month	Total
Bid and Proposal			
Beginning balance			
Current month's costs			
Supplies			
Engineering labor			
Service overhead			
Totals	$	$	$
Design			
Beginning balance			
Current month's costs			
Supplies			
Engineering labor			
Service overhead			
Totals	$	$	$
Prototype Development			
Beginning balance			
Current month's costs			
Special materials			
Engineering labor			
Service overhead			
Totals	$	$	$

Cost Summary to Date:	Total Cost
Bid and Proposal	$
Design	
Prototype Development	
Totals	$
Profit margin	
Contract revenue	$

Name ____________________

JOB ORDER COST CARD

Nedeau Engineering Co.

Customer: Customer B

Job Order No.: P–15

Product: Cost-Plus

Specs: ____________ Date Completed: Jan. 31, 20xx

Costs Charged to Job	Previous Months	Current Month	Total
Bid and Proposal			
Beginning balance			
Current month's costs			
Supplies			
Engineering labor			
Service overhead			
Totals	$	$	$
Design			
Beginning balance			
Current month's costs			
Supplies			
Engineering labor			
Service overhead			
Totals	$	$	$
Prototype Development			
Beginning balance			
Current month's costs			
Special materials			
Engineering labor			
Service overhead			
Totals	$	$	$

Cost Summary to Date:	Total Cost
Bid and Proposal	$
Design	
Prototype Development	
Totals	$
Profit margin	
Total contract revenue	$

Name

2.	Customer's cost per unit
3.	Ending Contract in Process Inventory balance

JOB ORDER COST CARD

Nedeau Engineering Co.

Customer: Customer C

Job Order No.: P–19

Contract Type: Cost-Plus

Specs:

Date Completed:

Costs Charged to Job	Previous Months	Current Month	Total
Bid and Proposal			
Beginning balance			
Current month's costs			
Supplies			
Engineering labor			
Service overhead			
Totals	$	$	$
Design			
Beginning balance			
Current month's costs			
Supplies			
Engineering labor			
Service overhead			
Totals	$	$	$
Prototype Development			
Beginning balance			
Current month's costs			
Special materials			
Engineering labor			
Service overhead			
Totals	$	$	$

Cost Summary to Date:	Total Cost
Bid and Proposal	$
Design	
Prototype Development	
Totals	$
Profit margin	
Contract revenue	$

2.	Customer's cost per unit computed
Customer A	
Customer B	
3.	Ending Contract-in-Process balance

Name ____________________

Chapter 17, P 5. Job Order Costing: Service Company

1. Job order cost cards created
2. Total cost calculated
3. Cost per attendee calculated

JOB ORDER COST CARD

Client: Monday Club

	Last Month's Cost	Current Month's Cost	Total Cost
Food and Beverage			
Labor			
Facility Overhead			
Total			
Number Served			
Cost per Attendee			

JOB ORDER COST CARD

Client: Huang-Smith

	Last Month's Cost	Current Month's Cost	Total Cost
Food and Beverage			
Labor			
Facility Overhead			
Total			
Number Served			
Cost per Attendee			

JOB ORDER COST CARD

Client: President Reception

	Last Month's Cost	Current Month's Cost	Total Cost
Food and Beverage			
Labor			
Facility Overhead			
Total			
Number Served			
Cost per Attendee			

Name

4.	Jobs ranked and observations made

Ranking:

Most to least costly:

Total Cost			Cost per Attendee	

Observations:

5.	Price charged discussed

Form is not provided; student should use his/her own paper.

Name

Chapter 17, P 6. Job Order Costing: T Account Analysis

1. Entries recorded in T accounts

Materials Inventory Control

Work in Process Inventory Control

Finished Goods Inventory Control

Manufacturing Overhead Control

Job A

Accounts Payable

Accounts Receivable

Name

1 (concluded)

Job B

Cost of Goods Sold

Job C

Property Taxes Payable

Selling and Administrative Expense

Factory Labor

Cash

Sales

Accumulated Depreciation, Manufacturing Equipment

Name

2. Underapplied overhead computed

Manufacturing overhead incurred

Manufacturing overhead applied

Underapplied overhead

Manufacturing Overhead Control

Cost of Goods Sold

Chapter 17, P 7. Job Order Cost Flow

1. Transactions reconstructed using T accounts
4. Ending inventory balances computed

Materials Inventory Control

Finished Goods Inventory Control

Manufacturing Overhead Control

Work in Process Inventory Control

Payroll Payable

Cost of Goods Sold

Sales

Accounts Receivable

Ending Work in Process Inventory Control:

Job AJ–10

Job AJ–14

Job AJ–30

Job AJ–16

Total

Name

2. Cost of completed units computed

Cost of ending Work in Process Inventory Control:

Job No.	Direct Materials	Direct Labor	Manufacturing Overhead	Total
AJ–10				
AJ–14				
AJ–30				
AJ–16				

Costs of units completed:

3. Cost of units sold computed

5.	Product unit costs computed

Job AJ–10:	
Job AJ–14:	

Chapter 17, P 8. Job Order Costing: Service Company

1. Job order cost cards created

JOB ORDER COST CARD

Napier & Associates
Homewood, Illinois

Customer: Adams, Inc. Date of Completion:

Costs Charged to Job	Previous Months	Current Month	Total Cost
Preliminary Analysis			
Beginning balance			
Current month's costs			
Supplies			
Labor			
Service overhead			
Totals	$	$	$
Field Work			
Beginning balance			
Current month's costs			
Supplies			
Labor			
Service overhead			
Totals	$	$	$
Report Development			
Beginning balance			
Current month's costs			
Supplies			
Labor			
Service overhead			
Totals	$	$	$

Cost Summary to Date	Total Cost
Preliminary Analysis	$
Field Work	
Report Development	
Totals	$
Profit margin	
Total contract revenue	

1 (continued)

JOB ORDER COST CARD

Napier & Associates
Homewood, Illinois

Customer: Brodahl Bakeries — Date of Completion: March 31, 20xx

Costs Charged to Job	Previous Months	Current Month	Total Cost
Preliminary Analysis			
Beginning balance			
Current month's costs			
Supplies			
Labor			
Service overhead			
Totals	$	$	$
Field Work			
Beginning balance			
Current month's costs			
Supplies			
Labor			
Service overhead			
Totals	$	$	$
Report Development			
Beginning balance			
Current month's costs			
Supplies			
Labor			
Service overhead			
Totals	$	$	$

Cost Summary to Date	Total Cost
Preliminary Analysis	$
Field Work	
Report Development	
Totals	$
Profit margin	
Total contract revenue	$

1 (concluded)

JOB ORDER COST CARD

Napier & Associates
Homewood, Illinois

Customer: Hill House Restaurants **Date of Completion:** March 31, 20xx

Costs Charged to Job	Previous Months	Current Month	Total Cost
Preliminary Analysis			
Beginning balance			
Current month's costs			
Supplies			
Labor			
Service overhead			
Totals	$	$	$
Field Work			
Beginning balance			
Current month's costs			
Supplies			
Labor			
Service overhead			
Totals	$	$	$
Report Development			
Beginning balance			
Current month's costs			
Supplies			
Labor			
Service overhead			
Totals	$	$	$

Cost Summary to Date	Total Cost
Preliminary Analysis	$
Field Work	
Report Development	
Totals	$
Profit margin	
Total contract revenue	

2.	Customer's cost per unit computed
Brodahl Bakeries	
Hill House Restaurants	
3.	Ending Contract-in-Process balance

Name

Chapter 18, SE 1. Process Versus Job Order Costing

1.
2.
3.
4.

Chapter 18, SE 2. Process Versus Job Order Costing

1.
2.
3.
4.
5.
6.

Chapter 18, SE 3. Process Costing and the Work in Process Inventory Account

Name

Chapter 18, SE 4. Equivalent Production: No Beginning Inventory

Blue Blaze
Schedule of Equivalent Production
For the Month Ended July 31, 20xx

Units—Stage of Completion	Units to Be Accounted For	Equivalent Units: Direct Materials Costs	Equivalent Units: Conversion Costs

Chapter 18, SE 5. Equivalent Production: Beginning Inventory

Units—Stage of Completion	Units to Be Accounted For	Equivalent Units: Direct Materials Costs	Equivalent Units: Conversion Costs

Name

Chapter 18, SE 6. Unit Cost Determination

Total Cost Analysis	Costs from Beginning Inventory	Costs from Current Period	Total Costs to Be Accounted For

Computation of Equivalent Unit Costs	Costs from Current Period	Equivalent Units	Cost per Equivalent Unit

Name

Chapter 18, SE 7. Cost Summary Schedule

Blue Blaze Cost Summary Schedule For the Month Ended July 31, 20xx			
	Cost of Goods Transferred to Finished Goods Inventory	Cost of Ending Work in Process Inventory	Total Costs to Be Accounted For

Chapter 18, SE 8. ABC and Process Costing

Conversion costs	
Total conversion costs	

Name

Chapter 18, SE 9. Measuring Performance with Product Costing Data

Chapter 18, SE 10. Average Costing Method

Peretti Pasta Company
Schedule of Equivalent Production
For the Year Ended July 31, 20xx

Units—Stage of Completion	Units to Be Accounted For	Equivalent Units Direct Materials Costs	Conversion Costs

Name

Chapter 18, E 1. Process Versus Job Order Costing

1.
2.
3.
4.
5.
6.
7.
8.

Chapter 18, E 2. Use of Process Costing Information

Chapter 18, E 3. Work in Process Inventory Accounting in Process Costing Systems

1.

2.

3.

4.

Chapter 18, E 4. Equivalent Units: No Beginning Inventories

Salazar Stone Company
Schedule of Equivalent Production—FIFO Costing Approach
For the Year Ended December 31, 20xx

Units—Stage of Completion	Units to Be Accounted For	Equivalent Units	
		Direct Materials Costs	Conversion Costs

Chapter 18, E 5. Equivalent Units: Beginning Inventories—FIFO Method

Zwick Enterprises
Schedule of Equivalent Production—FIFO Costing Approach
For the Month Ended January 31, 20xx

Units—Stage of Completion	Units to Be Accounted For	Equivalent Units	
		Direct Materials Costs	Conversion Costs

Name

Chapter 18, E 6. Work in Process Inventory Accounts: Total Unit Costs

	Direct Materials Costs			Conversion Costs			Total
Dept.	Dollars	Equiv. Units	Unit Cost	Dollars	Equiv. Units	Unit Cost	Unit Cost
A	12000 —	1,000	12 —	33825 —	2,050	16 50	28 50
B							
C							
D							
E							
Totals							

Chapter 18, E 7. Unit Cost Determination

Neff Kitchenwares, Inc.
Unit Cost Analysis Schedule—FIFO Costing Approach
For the Month Ended July 31, 20xx

Total Cost Analysis	Costs from Beginning Inventory	Current Period Costs	Total Costs to Be Accounted For

Computation of Equivalent Unit Costs	Current Period Costs	Equivalent Units	Cost per Equivalent Unit

Name

Chapter 18, E 8. Cost Summary Schedule

Kristoff Bakery Cost Summary Schedule—FIFO Costing Approach For the Month Ended August 31, 20xx			
	Cost of Goods Transferred to Finished Goods Inventory	Cost of Ending Work in Process Inventory	Total Costs to Be Accounted For

Name

Chapter 18, E 9. ABC and Product Unit Cost

ABC-assigned overhead for the Lithograph Work Cell computed

Activity	Cost Driver Level		Assignment Rate		Cost Assigned
Engineering design	25	engineering hours	$ 68.00	per engineering hour	
Design layouts	80	design hours	120.00	per design hour	
Layout setups	6	setups	210.00	per setup	
Materials purchasing	9	purchases	330.00	per purchase	
Companywide overhead	650	square feet	3.20	per square foot	
Total overhead costs assigned					

Unit cost analysis schedule prepared

Golden Enterprises
Unit Cost Analysis Schedule
For the Month Ended August 31, 20xx

Total Cost Analysis	Costs from Beginning Inventory	Current Period Costs	Total Costs to Be Accounted For

Name

E 9 (continued)

Computation of Equivalent Unit Costs	Costs from Current Period	Equivalent Units	Cost per Equivalent Unit

Chapter 18, E 10. Measuring Performance with Nonfinancial Product Data

Form is not provided; student should use his/her own paper.

Chapter 18, E 11. Average Costing Method

Schedule of equivalent production, unit cost analysis schedule, and cost summary schedule prepared

Uncle Fun Corporation
Toy Truck Work Cell
Process Cost Report Using Average Costing
For the Month Ended July 31, 20xx

	Units to Be Accounted For	Equivalent Units	
Units—Stage of Completion		Direct Materials Costs	Conversion Costs

Name

E 11 (continued)

Unit cost analysis schedule

	(1) Costs from Beginning Inventory	(2) Current Period Costs	(3) Total Costs to Be Accounted For	(4) Equivalent Units	(3 ÷ 4) Cost per Equivalent Unit

Name

E 11 (concluded)

Cost Summary Schedule

	Cost of Goods Transferred to Finished Goods Inventory	Cost of Ending Work in Process Inventory	Total Costs to Be Accounted For

Chapter 18, P 1. Process Costing: No Beginning Inventories

1. Schedule of equivalent production, unit cost analysis schedule, and cost summary schedule prepared

Cee Gee Chewing Gum Company
Blending Department
Process Cost Report
For the Month Ended June 30, 20xx

1a. Schedule of equivalent production

Units—Stage of Completion	Units to Be Accounted For	Equivalent Units: Direct Materials Costs	Equivalent Units: Conversion Costs

Name

1b. Unit cost analysis schedule

Total Cost Analysis	Costs from Beginning Inventory	Current Period Costs	Total Costs to Be Accounted For

Computation of Equivalent Unit Costs	Current Period Costs	Equivalent Units	Cost per Equivalent Unit

1c. Cost summary schedule

	Cost of Goods Transferred to Packing Department	Cost of Ending Work in Process Inventory	Total Costs to Be Accounted For

2. Amount to be transferred

Name

Chapter 18, P 2. Process Costing: With Beginning Inventories—FIFO Method

1. Schedule of equivalent production, unit cost analysis schedule, and cost summary schedule prepared

Waukesha Bottling Company
Mixing Department
Process Cost Report
For the Month Ended August 31, 20xx

1a. Schedule of equivalent production

Units—Stage of Completion	Units to Be Accounted For	Equivalent Units Direct Materials Costs	Equivalent Units Conversion Costs

1b. Unit cost analysis schedule

Total Cost Analysis	Costs from Beginning Inventory	Current Period Costs	Total Costs to Be Accounted For

Computation of Equivalent Unit Costs	Current Period Costs	Equivalent Units	Cost per Equivalent Unit

Name

1c. Cost summary schedule

	Cost of Goods Transferred to Bottling Department	Cost of Ending Work in Process Inventory	Total Costs to Be Accounted For

2. Amount to be transferred

Name

Chapter 18, P 3. Process Costing: One Process/Two Time Periods—FIFO Method

A unit analysis may help in the solution to this problem.

	April	May

Name

P 3 (continued)

1. **Schedule of equivalent production, unit cost analysis schedule, and cost summary schedule prepared**

Verdant Valley Company
Process Cost Report
For the Month Ended April 30, 20xx

1a. Schedule of equivalent production

Units—Stage of Completion	Units to Be Accounted For	Equivalent Units: Direct Materials Costs	Equivalent Units: Conversion Costs

1b. Unit cost analysis schedule

Total Cost Analysis	Costs from Beginning Inventory	Current Period Costs	Total Costs to Be Accounted For

Computation of Equivalent Unit Costs	Current Period Costs	Equivalent Units	Cost per Equivalent Unit

1c. Cost summary schedule			
	Cost of Goods Transferred to Finished Goods Inventory	Cost of Ending Work in Process Inventory	Total Costs to Be Accounted For

2. Amount to be transferred

Name

P 3 (continued)

3. Schedule of equivalent production, unit cost analysis schedule, and cost summary schedule prepared

Verdant Valley Company
Process Cost Report
For the Month Ended May 31, 20xx

3a. Schedule of equivalent production

Units—Stage of Completion	Units to Be Accounted For	Equivalent Units	
		Direct Materials Costs	Conversion Costs

3b. Unit cost analysis schedule

Total Cost Analysis	Costs from Beginning Inventory	Current Period Costs	Total Costs to Be Accounted For

Computation of Equivalent Unit Costs	Current Period Costs	Equivalent Units	Cost per Equivalent Unit

Name

3c. Cost summary schedule

	Cost of Goods Transferred to Finished Goods Inventory	Cost of Ending Work in Process Inventory	Total Costs to Be Accounted For

4. Amount to be transferred

Name ____________________

Chapter 18, P 4. Process Costing System and ABC

1. Activity-based cost assignment rates computed

Activity	Cost Driver	Cost Driver Level	Total Cost	Assignment Rate
Materials purchasing	Number of purchase orders			per purchase order
Machine repairs	Repair hours			per hour
Machine setups	Number of setups			per setup
Materials moving	Number of moves			per move
Companywide overhead	Number of square feet			per square foot

2. ABC overhead assigned to Bonding Work Cell computed

Activity	Cost Driver Level	Assignment Rate	Cost Assigned
Materials purchasing	purchase orders		
Machine repairs	repair hours		
Machine setups	setups		
Materials moving	moves		
Companywide overhead	square feet		
Total overhead costs assigned			

P 4 (continued)

3. **Schedule of equivalent production, unit cost analysis schedule, and cost summary schedule prepared**

Huizinga Company
Product Bonding Work Cell
Process Cost Report
For the Month Ended July 31, 20xx

a. Schedule of equivalent production

Units—Stage of Completion	Units to Be Accounted For	Equivalent Units: Direct Materials Costs	Equivalent Units: Conversion Costs

Name

b. Unit cost analysis schedule

Total Cost Analysis	Costs from Beginning Inventory	Current Period Costs	Total Costs to Be Accounted For

Computation of Equivalent Unit Costs	Current Period Costs	Equivalent Units	Cost per Equivalent Unit

Name

c. Cost summary schedule	Cost of Goods Transferred to Packaging Work Cell	Cost of Ending Work in Process Inventory	Total Costs to Be Accounted For

Name

Chapter 18, P 5. Process Costing: With Beginning Inventories/ Two Departments—FIFO Method

A unit analysis may help in the solution to this problem.

	Mixing Department	Cooking Department

Name

P 5 (continued)

1. Schedule of equivalent production, unit cost analysis schedule, and cost summary schedule prepared

Freeland Foods, Inc.
Mixing Department
Process Cost Report
For the Month Ended January 31, 20xx

1a. Schedule of equivalent production

	Units to Be Accounted For	Equivalent Units	
Units—Stage of Completion		Direct Materials Costs	Conversion Costs

Name

1b. Unit cost analysis schedule

Total Cost Analysis	Costs from Beginning Inventory	Current Period Costs	Total Costs to Be Accounted For

Computation of Equivalent Unit Costs	Current Period Costs	Equivalent Units	Cost per Equivalent Unit

Name

1c. Cost summary schedule	Cost of Goods Transferred to Cooking Department	Cost of Ending Work in Process Inventory	Total Costs to Be Accounted For

Name

P 5 (continued)

2. **Schedule of equivalent production, unit cost analysis schedule, and cost summary schedule prepared**

Freeland Foods, Inc.
Cooking Department
Process Cost Report
For the Month Ended January 31, 20xx

2a. Schedule of equivalent production

Units—Stage of Completion	Units to Be Accounted For	Equivalent Units	
		Transferred-in Costs	Conversion Costs

Name

2b. Unit cost analysis schedule

Total Cost Analysis	Costs from Beginning Inventory	Current Period Costs	Total Costs to Be Accounted For

Computation of Equivalent Unit Costs	Current Period Costs	Equivalent Units	Cost per Equivalent Unit

Name

2c. Cost summary schedule			
	Cost of Goods Transferred to Canning Department	Cost of Ending Work in Process Inventory	Total Costs to Be Accounted For

Chapter 18, P 6. Process Costing: With Beginning Inventories—FIFO Method

1. Schedule of equivalent production, unit cost analysis schedule, and cost summary schedule prepared

Lacho Liquid Extracts Company
Process Cost Report
For the Month Ended June 30, 20xx

1a. Schedule of equivalent production

	Units	Equivalent Units	
	to Be	Direct	
	Accounted	Materials	Conversion
Units—Stage of Completion	For	Costs	Costs

1b. Unit cost analysis schedule

Total Cost Analysis	Costs from Beginning Inventory	Current Period Costs	Total Costs to Be Accounted For

Computation of Equivalent Unit Costs	Current Period Costs	Equivalent Units	Cost per Equivalent Unit

1c. Cost summary schedule			
	Cost of Goods Transferred to Finished Goods Inventory	Cost of Ending Work in Process Inventory	Total Costs to Be Accounted For

2.	Amount to be transferred

Name

Chapter 18, P 7. Process Costing: One Process/Two Time Periods—FIFO Method

A unit analysis may help in the solution to this problem.

	July	August

Name

P 7 (continued)

1. **Schedule of equivalent production, unit cost analysis schedule, and cost summary schedule prepared**

Coconino Laboratories
Process Cost Report
For the Month Ended July 31, 20xx

1a. Schedule of equivalent production

	Units to Be Accounted For	Equivalent Units	
Units—Stage of Completion		Direct Materials Costs	Conversion Costs

1b. Unit cost analysis schedule

Total Cost Analysis	Costs from Beginning Inventory	Current Period Costs	Total Costs to Be Accounted For

Computation of Equivalent Unit Costs	Current Period Costs	Equivalent Units	Cost per Equivalent Unit

1c. Cost summary schedule	Cost of Goods Transferred to Finished Goods Inventory	Cost of Ending Work in Process Inventory	Total Costs to Be Accounted For

2. Amount to be transferred

Name

P 7 (continued)

3. Schedule of equivalent production, unit cost analysis schedule, and cost summary schedule prepared

Coconino Laboratories
Process Cost Report
For the Month Ended August 31, 20xx

3a. Schedule of equivalent production

Units—Stage of Completion	Units to Be Accounted For	Equivalent Units	
		Direct Materials Costs	Conversion Costs

3b. Unit cost analysis schedule

Total Cost Analysis	Costs from Beginning Inventory	Current Period Costs	Total Costs to Be Accounted For

Computation of Equivalent Unit Costs	Current Period Costs	Equivalent Units	Cost per Equivalent Unit

Name

3c. Cost summary schedule

	Cost of Goods Transferred to Finished Goods Inventory	Cost of Ending Work in Process Inventory	Total Costs to Be Accounted For

4. Amount to be transferred

Chapter 18, P 8. Process Costing: With Beginning Inventories—Average Costing Method

1.	Schedule of equivalent production, unit cost analysis schedule, and cost summary schedule prepared

Hi-E Food Products, Inc.
Process Cost Report Using Average Costing
For the Month Ended February 28, 20xx

1a. Schedule of equivalent production

Units—Stage of Completion	Units to Be Accounted For	Equivalent Units: Direct Materials Costs	Equivalent Units: Conversion Costs

P 8 (continued)

1b. Unit cost analysis schedule

	Total Costs			Equivalent Unit Costs	
	(1) Costs from Beginning Inventory	(2) Current Period Costs	(3) Total Costs to Be Accounted For	(4) Equivalent Units	(3 ÷ 4) Cost per Equivalent Unit

P 8 (concluded)

1c. Cost Summary Schedule

	Cost of Goods Transferred to Finished Goods Inventory	Cost of Ending Work in Process Inventory	Total Costs to Be Accounted For

2. Amount to be transferred

Name

Chapter 19, SE 1. Activity-Based Systems
Form is not provided; student should use his/her own paper.

Chapter 19, SE 2. Identifying a Product's Value Chain
Form is not provided; student should use his/her own paper.

Chapter 19, SE 3. Supply Chain
Form is not provided; student should use his/her own paper.

Chapter 19, SE 4. Value-Adding Versus Nonvalue-Adding Activities
Form is not provided; student should use his/her own paper.

Chapter 19, SE 5. ABC Cost Hierarchy
1.
2.
3.

Chapter 19, SE 6. Elements of a JIT Operating Environment
Form is not provided; student should use his/her own paper.

Chapter 19, SE 7. Product Costing Changes in a JIT Environment
Storage barrels for work in process inventory:
Inspection labor:
Machine electricity:
Machine repairs:
Depreciation of the storage barrel movers:
Machine setup labor:

Chapter 19, SE 8. Backflush Costing

Name

Chapter 19, SE 9. ABM and JIT Compared

Form is not provided; student should use his/her own paper.

Chapter 19, E 1. Supply Chains and Value Chains

Plant and tree vendor	Advertising company manager
Purchasing potted trees	Scheduling delivery trucks
Computer and software salesperson	Customer service
Creating marketing plans	

Chapter 19, E 2. Process Value Analysis

Chapter 19, E 3. ABC Cost Hierarchy

New product design	Sales commissions
Product line marketing	Bulk packing of orders
Unique system design	Assembly labor costs
Unique system packaging	Assembly line setup
Direct materials costs	Securing the building
Repairing the building	Product line supervision

Chapter 19, E 4. Elements of JIT

1.	5.
2.	6.
3.	7.
4.	

Name ______________________

Chapter 19, E 5. Direct Versus Indirect Costs

1. Costs in a traditional manufacturing setting identified
2. Costs in a JIT environment identified

	Traditional Setting	Costs That Are the Same in Both JIT and Traditional Settings	Costs That Change in a JIT Environment	Reason for the Change
Direct materials				
Sheet steel				
Iron castings				
Assembly parts				
Part 24RE6				
Part 15RF8				
Direct labor				
Engineering labor				
Indirect labor				
Operating supplies				
Small tools				
Depreciation, plant				
Depreciation, machinery				
Supervisory salaries				
Electrical power				
Insurance and taxes,				
plant				
President's salary				
Employee benefits				

Name

Chapter 19, E 6. Raw in Process Inventory

Name

Chapter 19, E 7. Backflush Costing

Accounts Payable

Cost of Goods Sold

Conversion Costs

Costs remaining in Raw in Process Inventory at month end backflushed

Raw in Process Inventory

Factory Payroll

Costs remaining in Finished Goods Inventory at month end backflushed

Manufacturing Overhead

Finished Goods Inventory

Chapter 19, E 8. ABM Versus JIT

1.
2.
3.
4.
5.

Name

Chapter 19, P 1. Value Chain and Process Value Analysis	
1.	Non-value-adding activities identified
2.	Value-adding activities grouped into the seven categories of the value chain
Marketing:	
Research and development:	
Purchasing:	
Production:	
Sales:	
Shipping:	
Customer service:	
3.	Necessary and unnecessary nonvalue-adding activities identified
(Form is not provided; student should use his/her own paper.)	

Name

Chapter 19, P 2. ABM and Activity-Based Costing

1.	Traditional costing approach applied to job

Life Spring Order:	
Product unit cost (total cost ÷ 150 units)	

2.	Cost hierarchy identified

Unit level:
Batch level:
Product level:
Facility level:

P 2 (concluded)

3 and 4.	Bill of activities and activity-based costing applied to job

Kalina Products, Inc.
Bill of Activities
Life Spring Order

Activity/Cost Pool	Cost Pool Rate	Cost Driver Level	Activity Cost
Unit level			
	per		
	per		
	per		
Batch level			
	per		
Product level			
	per		
Facility level			
	per		
Total activity costs assigned to job			
Total units of job			
Activity costs per unit (total activity costs ÷ total units)			
Cost summary			
Activity costs			
Direct materials cost			
Costs of purchased parts			
Direct labor cost			
Total cost of order			
Product unit cost (total cost ÷ 150 units)			

5.	Costs compared

Product unit cost—traditional costing approach	
Product unit cost—activity-based costing approach	
Difference	

Comparison explained.

Form is not provided; student should use his/her own paper.

Chapter 19, P 3. Product Costing in a JIT Work Cell

1a. Materials handling cost allocation rate computed

Materials	
Leather	25430 —
Metal frame	39180 —
Bolts	3010 —
Total materials cost	
Materials handling	
Labor	8232 —
Equipment depreciation	4410 —
Electrical power	2460 —
Maintenance	5184 —
Total materials handling cost	
Materials handling cost allocation rate	

1b. Engineering design cost allocation rate computed

Engineering design	
Labor	4116 —
Electrical power	1176 —
Engineering overhead	7644 —
Total engineering design cost	
Engineering design cost allocation rate	

P 3 (concluded)

1c. **JIT overhead allocation rate computed**

JIT overhead	
Equipment depreciation	7056 —
Indirect labor	30870 —
Supervision	17640 —
Operating supplies	4410 —
Electrical power	10584 —
Repairs and maintenance	21168 —
Building occupancy overhead	52920 —
Total JIT overhead cost	
Machine hours	
JIT overhead allocation rate	

2. **Product unit cost of one bicycle seat computed**

Materials cost	
Materials handling cost	
Direct labor cost	
Engineering design cost	
JIT overhead cost	
Manufacturing cost per seat	

Name

Chapter 19, P 4. Backflush Costing

1. JIT cost flow diagrammed

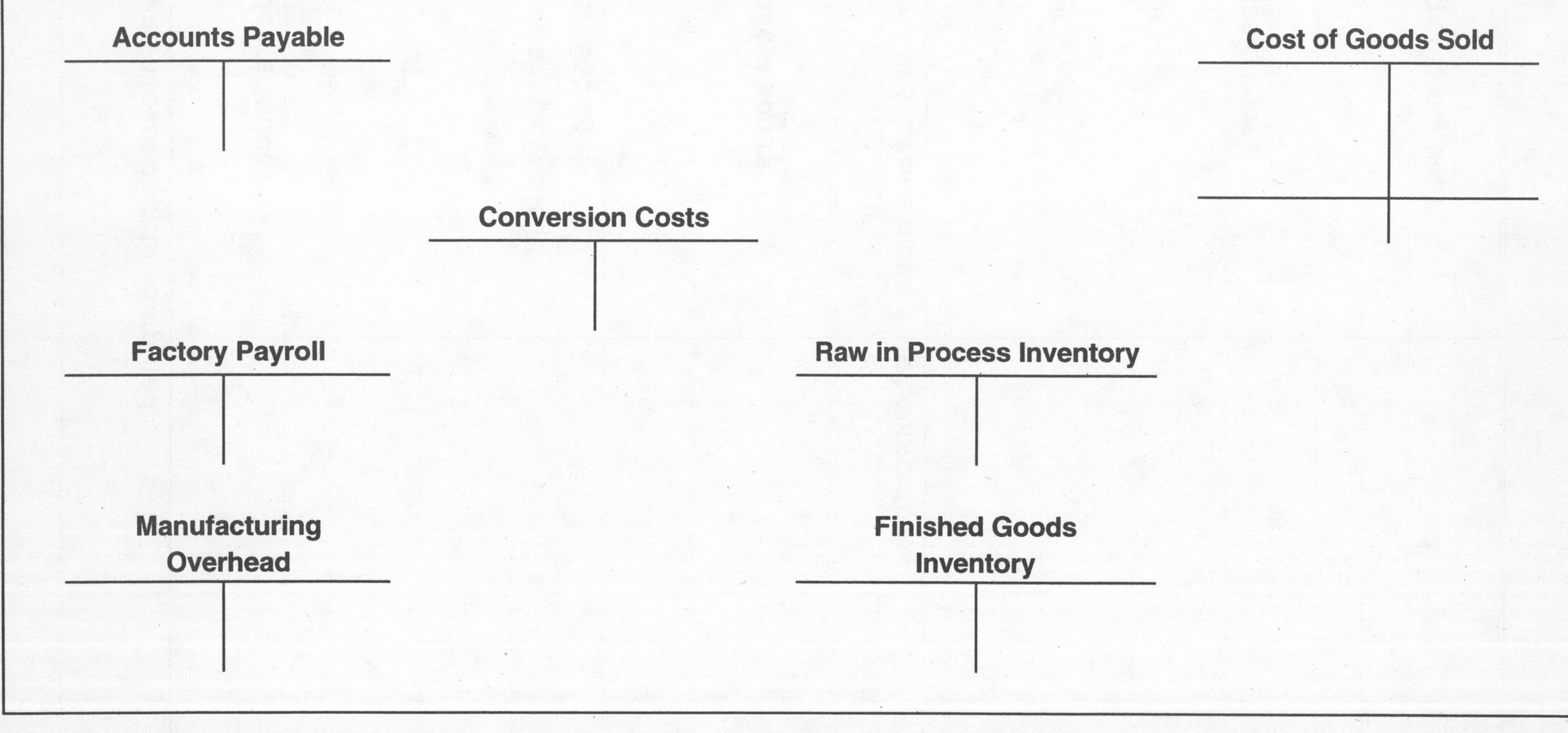

P 4 (concluded)

2. Traditional cost flow diagrammed

Accounts Payable

Materials Inventory

Work in Process Inventory

Finished Goods Inventory

Factory Payroll

Cost of Goods Sold

Manufacturing Overhead

3. The cost of goods sold for April is ____________.

Name

Chapter 19, P 5. Activities and Activity-Based Costing

1. Traditional costing approach applied to job

Johanna Order:	
Direct materials costs	
Cost of purchased parts	
Direct labor cost	
Manufacturing overhead	
Total cost of order	
Product unit cost	

2. Cost hierarchy identified

Unit level:

Batch level:

Product level:

Facility level:

P 5 (concluded)

3 and 4. Bill of activities and activity-based costing applied to job

Crampton Cellular Company
Bill of Activities
Johanna Order

Activity/Cost Pool	Cost Pool Rate		Cost Driver Level		Activity Cost
Unit level					
		per			
		per			
Batch level					
		per			
Product level					
		per			
		per			
Facility level					
		per			
Total activity costs assigned to job					
Total units of job					
Activity costs per unit (total activity costs ÷ total units)					
Cost summary					
Activity costs					
Direct materials cost					
Costs of purchased parts					
Direct labor cost					
Total cost of order					
Product unit cost (total cost ÷ 80 units)					

5. Costs compared

Product unit cost—traditional costing approach	
Product unit cost—activity-based costing approach	
Difference	

Comparison explained.
Form is not provided; student should use his/her own paper.

Name

Chapter 19, P 6. Backflush Accounting

1. JIT cost flow

Accounts Payable

Cost of Goods Sold

Conversion Costs

Raw in Process Inventory

Factory Payroll

Manufacturing Overhead

Finished Goods Inventory

Name ____________

P 6 (concluded)

2. Traditional cost flow

Accounts Payable

Materials Inventory

Work in Process Inventory

Finished Goods Inventory

Factory Payroll

Cost of Goods Sold

Manufacturing Overhead

3. The cost of goods sold for February is ________.

Name

Chapter 20, SE 1. Concepts of Cost Behavior

Hat maker A:

Hat maker B:

Chapter 20, SE 2. Identification of Variable, Fixed, and Mixed Costs

1.
2.
3.
4.
5.

Chapter 20, SE 3. Mixed Costs: High-Low Method

Volume	Month	Activity Level	Cost

Name

Chapter 20, SE 4. Cost-Volume-Profit Analysis

Chapter 20, SE 5. Computing the Breakeven Point

Chapter 20, SE 6. Contribution Margin

Chapter 20, SE 7. Cost-Volume-Profit Analysis for Multiple Products

Chapter 20, SE 8. Contribution Margin and Projected Profit

Chapter 20, SE 9. Cost Behavior in a Service Business

Volume	Month	Activity Level	Cost

Chapter 20, E 1. Identification of Variable and Fixed Costs

1.	9.
2.	10.
3.	11.
4.	12.
5.	13.
6.	14.
7.	15.
8.	16.

Chapter 20, E 2. Variable Cost Analysis

1. Cost of oil computed

Month	Cars to Be Serviced	Required Quarts/Car	Cost/Quart	Total Cost/Month
1	240	4	$0.50	
2	288	4	0.50	
3	360	4	0.50	
Three-month total	888			

2. Information about cost behavior provided

Cost per unit ______________________________.

Total variable cost per month ____________________ as the quantity

of oil used ____________________.

Name ______________________

Chapter 20, E 3. Mixed Costs: High-Low Method

1. Variable electricity cost per machine hour computed

Volume	Month	Machine Hours	Electricity Cost

Variable rate =

2. Monthly fixed electricity cost computed

3. Total variable and fixed electricity costs for six months computed

Chapter 20, E 4. Graphical Analysis

1.
2.
3.
4.
5.
6.

Chapter 20, E 5. Breakeven Analysis

1. Breakeven units computed

BE units	=	
	=	
	=	
	=	

2. Breakeven dollars computed

BE dollars	=	
	=	
	=	

3. New breakeven units computed

BE units	=	
	=	
	=	
	=	

Name ______________________

E 5 (continued)

4. Breakeven graph prepared

Units	Fixed Costs	Variable Costs	Total Costs	Total Sales

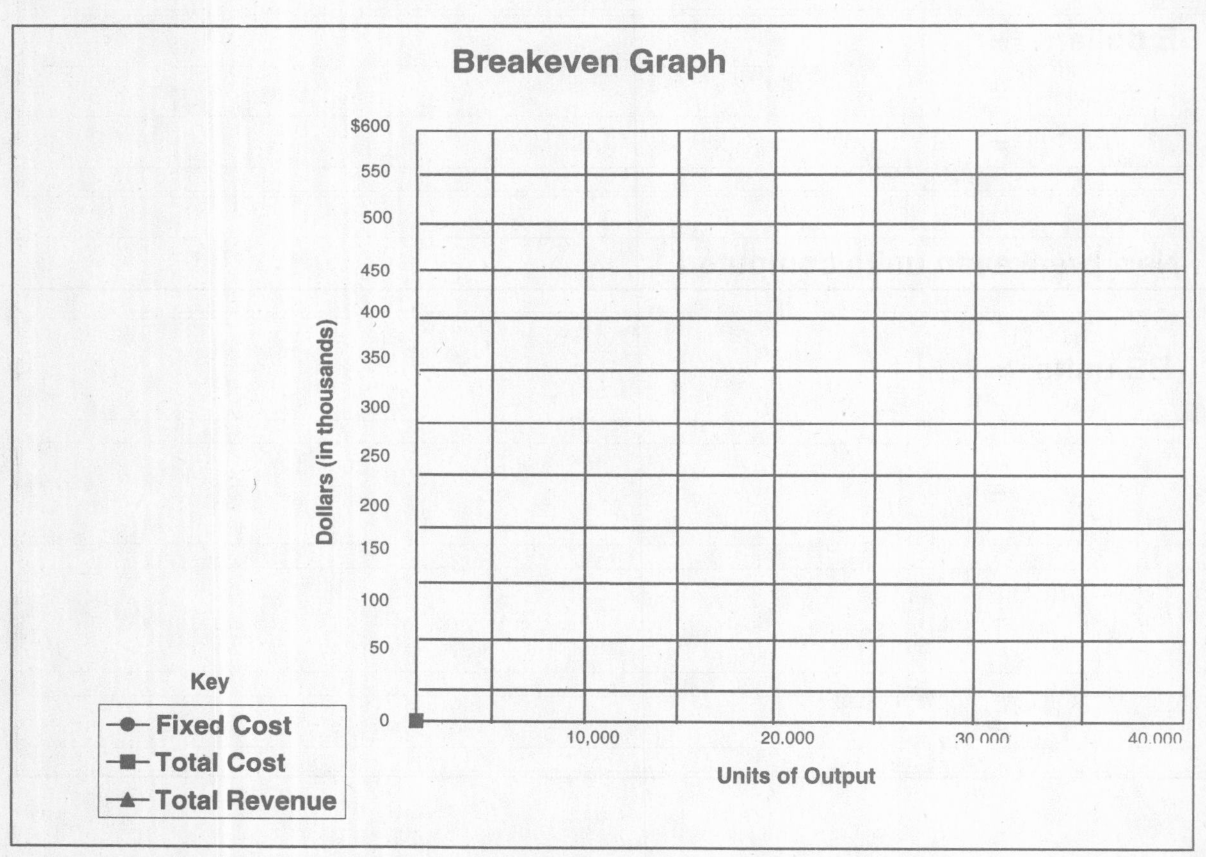

Name ______________________

Chapter 20, E 6. Calculate Breakeven Point for Multiple Products

	Sales	–	Variable Costs	=	Contribution Margin (CM)	x	Percentage of Sales Mix	=	Weighted-Average CM
Aquariums		–		=		x		=	
Water pumps		–		=		x		=	
Air filters		–		=		x		=	
Weighted-average contribution margin									

Weighted-average breakeven point =

Breakeven point for each product:

Aquariums

Water pumps

Air filters

Check: Contribution margin

Name

Chapter 20, E 7. Contribution Margin/Profit Planning		
1.	**Target sales units calculated**	
Target sales units	=	
	=	
	=	
	=	
2.	**Revised target sales units calculated**	
Target sales units	=	
	=	
	=	
	=	
	=	

3.	Additional units needed to earn higher net income calculated	
Additional units	=	
	=	
	=	
Proof:		
	=	
	=	
	=	
	=	

Chapter 20, E 8. Planning Future Sales

1. Target sales units calculated

Target sales units	=	
	=	
	=	
	=	

2. Target average number of rental days per auto per year computed

3. Target sales dollars computed

Target revenue	=	
	=	
	=	

4. Revised target sales dollars computed

Revised target sales dollars	=	
	=	
	=	
	=	
	=	

Name

Chapter 20, E 9. Cost Behavior in a Service Business

1. Variable and fixed cost components calculated

Volume	Month	Number of Tax Returns	Cost

2. Estimated total cost per tax return in April calculated

Name

Chapter 20, P 1. Cost Behavior and Projection

1. Costs classified

Variable costs:

Fixed costs:

Mixed costs:

2. High-low method applied

Volume	Month	Number of Jobs	Utilities Cost

3 and 4. Projected total costs and projected cost per job computed

	Total Cost	Cost per Job
Variable costs:		
Fixed costs:		
Mixed costs:		

5. Decision about raising the price discussed

Name

Chapter 20, P 2. Breakeven Analysis

1. Breakeven hours computed

BE units	=	
	=	
	=	
	=	

2. Breakeven billings computed

BE dollars	=	
	=	
	=	

3. Breakeven billings revised based on higher fixed costs

BE dollars	=	
	=	
	=	
	=	
	=	

4. Breakeven billings revised based on new operating data

BE dollars	=	
	=	
	=	
	=	
	=	

Chapter 20, P 3. Planning Future Sales

1a. Breakeven number of applications computed

BE units	=	
	=	
	=	

1b. Target number of applications computed

Target sales units	=	
	=	
	=	

2. Target number of applications computed based on new operating data

Target sales units	=	
	=	
	=	

Name

3.	Application fee determined	
x	=	loan application fee
Target revenue	=	
	=	
	=	
	=	
	=	
	=	

4.	Maximum additional promotional costs determined	
x	=	maximum additional promotional costs
Target revenue	=	
	=	
	=	
	=	
	=	
	=	
	=	

Name

Chapter 20, P 4. Planning Future Sales

1a and 1b.	Breakeven units and dollars computed

BE units	=	
	=	
	=	
	=	
BE dollars	=	
	=	

2.	Target sales units computed

Target sales units	=	
	=	
	=	
	=	

Name

3.	Contribution margin per unit computed	
a.		
b.		=
		=
		=
		=

Name ______________________

Chapter 20, P 5. Breakeven Analysis

1. Breakeven units computed

BE units	=	
	=	
	=	
	=	

2. Breakeven dollars computed

BE dollars	=	
	=	
	=	

3. Breakeven units revised based on higher fixed costs

BE units	=	
	=	
	=	
	=	

4. Breakeven units revised based on new operating data

BE units	=	
	=	
	=	
	=	
	=	

Name ______________________

Chapter 20, P 6. Planning Future Sales: Contribution Margin Approach

1a. Breakeven units computed

BE units	=	
	=	
	=	
	=	
	=	

1b. Target units computed

Target sales units	=	
	=	
	=	
	=	

2. Target sales units revised based on new operating data

Target sales units	=	
	=	
	=	
	=	

3. Selling price determined

x	=	revised selling price
Target sales units	=	

Multiplying both sides of the equation by (x − $28.60), we get

4. Increased advertising costs determined

Target sales units	=	

Name

Chapter 21, SE 1. Budgeting and the Management Cycle

1.
2.
3.
4.
5.

Chapter 21, SE 2. Manager's Budget Uses

Budgets that might be useful include:

1.

2.

3.

4.

5.

Chapter 21, SE 3. Budgetary Control

Form is not provided; student should use his/her own paper.

Chapter 21, SE 4. Budgeting Principles

Form is not provided; student should use his/her own paper.

Chapter 21, SE 5. Master Budget Components

Form is not provided; student should use his/her own paper.

Chapter 21, SE 6. Operating Budget Preparation

Chapter 21, SE 7. Operating Budget Preparation

Name

Chapter 21, SE 8. Budgeted Gross Margin

Cost of Goods Manufactured

Chapter 21, SE 9. Cash Budget

Martinson Corp. Schedule of Expected Cash Payments for Direct Materials For the Quarter Ended March 31, 20x1				
	January	February	March	Quarter

Chapter 21, SE 10. Budgeted Balance Sheet

Chapter 21, SE 11. Identification of Controllable Costs

1.	4.
2.	5.
3.	

Chapter 21, SE 12. Cost Centers, Profit Centers, and Investment Centers

1.

2.

Name

Chapter 21, E 1. Budgeting and the Management Cycle

1.
2.
3.
4.
5.
6.
7.
8.
9.
10.

Chapter 21, E 2. Budget Objectives

1.	
2.	
3.	
4.	

Chapter 21, E 3. Budgeting Principles

1.	
2.	

Chapter 21, E 4. Budgeting Principles

Chapter 21, E 5. Components of a Master Budget

1.
2.
3.
4.
5.
6.
7.

Chapter 21, E 6. Sales Budget Preparation

Crosson Manufacturing Company
Sales Budget
For the Year Ended December 31, 20x2

Product Class	January–March	April–June	July–September	October–December	Year
Marine Products					
Mountain Products					
River Products					
Hiking Products					
Running Products					
Biking Products					
Totals					

Name

Chapter 21, E 7. Production Budget Preparation

All-in-One Door Company
Production Budget
For the Quarter Ended March 31, 20xx

	January	February	March

Chapter 21, E 8. Direct Materials Purchases Budget

All-in-One Door Company
Direct Materials Purchases Budget
For the Quarter Ended March 31, 20xx

Number of Units to Be Produced: 16,000

	Quantity per Door	Cost per Quantity	Cost per Door	Total Direct Materials Cost

Name ______________________

Chapter 21, E 9. Direct Labor Budget Preparation

Whitmore Metals Company
Direct Labor Budget
For the Year Ended December 31, 20x1

Cutting Department	Product T	Product M	Product B	Year
Total Production Units				
x Direct Labor Hours per Unit				
Total Direct Labor Hours				
x Direct Labor Cost per Hour				
Total Direct Labor Cost				
Grinding Department	**Product T**	**Product M**	**Product B**	
Total Production Units				
x Direct Labor Hours per Unit				
Total Direct Labor Hours				
x Direct Labor Cost per Hour				
Total Direct Labor Cost				
Total Direct Labor Cost				

Name

Chapter 21, E 10. Manufacturing Overhead Budget

Name

Chapter 21, E 11. Cash Budget Preparation—Revenues

Purposes of a cash budget:

Magrone Car Care, Inc.
Schedule of Expected Cash Collections from Customers
For the Quarter Ended December 31, 20x1

	Credit Sales	October	November	December	Quarter

Name

Chapter 21, E 12. Identification of Controllable Costs

	Behavior	Controlled by
1.		
2.		
3.		
4.		
5.		
6.		
7.		
8.		
9.		
10.		
11.		

Name

Chapter 21, P 1. Budget Preparation

1. Monthly cost information prepared

	October	November	December

Name ____________________

2. Quarterly budget prepared

Cho Sun Enterprises, Inc.
Cost of Goods Manufactured Budget
For the Quarter Ended December 31, 20x1

	October	November	December	Quarter

Name

Chapter 21, P 2. Comprehensive Budgeted Income Statement

Operating budgets and budgeted income statement prepared

1. Sales Budget

Blue's Bath Oils
Sales Budget
For the Year Ended December 31, 20x2

	Quarter				
	1	2	3	4	Year

2. Production Budget

Blue's Bath Oils
Production Budget
For the Year Ended December 31, 20x2

	Quarter				
	1	2	3	4	Year

Note 1:	Desired units of ending finished goods inventory = 10% of *next* quarter's budgeted sales.
Note 2:	Desired units of beginning finished goods inventory = 10% of *current* quarter's budgeted sales.

3. Direct Materials Purchases Budget

Blue's Bath Oils
Direct Materials Purchases Budget
For the Year Ended December 31, 20x2

	Quarter				
	1	2	3	4	Year

Note 1:

Note 2:

Note 3:

4. Direct Labor Budget

Blue's Bath Oils
Direct Labor Budget
For the Year Ended December 31, 20x2

	Quarter				
	1	2	3	4	Year

Name ______________________

5. Manufacturing Overhead Budget

Blue's Bath Oils
Manufacturing Overhead Budget
For the Year Ended December 31, 20x2

	Quarter				
	1	2	3	4	Year

Name

6. Selling and Administrative Expense Budget

Blue's Bath Oils Selling and Administrative Expense Budget For the Year Ended December 31, 20x2					
	Quarter				
	1	2	3	4	Year

7. Cost of Goods Manufactured Budget

Blue's Bath Oils
Cost of Goods Manufactured Budget
For the Year Ended December 31, 20x2

Manufactured cost per unit =

***It is a company policy to have no units in process at year end.**

8. Budgeted Income Statement

Blue's Bath Oils
Budgeted Income Statement
For the Year Ended December 31, 20x2

Name

Chapter 21, P 3. Basic Cash Budget

Computation of cash receipts from credit sales:

	Total Credit Sales			Cash Receipts on Account		
Month	x Collection %			July	August	September
May		x				
		x				
		x				
		x				
		x				
		x				
		x				
		x				
		x				
Totals						

Name

1. Cash budget prepared

Produce Mart, Inc.
Monthly Cash Budgets
For the Quarter Ended September 30, 20x3

	July	August	September	Quarter

2. Loan possibility discussed

Name

Chapter 21, P 4. Budgeted Financial Statements

Preliminary schedules:

Name

1. Budgeted income statement prepared

Montoya Products, Inc.
Budgeted Income Statement
For the Quarter Ended June 30, 20x1

Name

2. Budgeted balance sheet prepared

Assets

Liabilities

Stockholders' Equity

Name

Chapter 21, P 5. Cash Budget Preparation: Comprehensive

Black Hills Ski Resort, Inc.
Cash Budget
For the Year Ended December 31, 20x2

Item	January	February	March	April–December	Year

Chapter 21, P 6. Budgeted Income Statement

1. 20x5 budgeted income statement prepared

Overland Spectaculars, Inc.
Budgeted Income Statement
For the Year Ended December 31, 20x5

2. Trend in company's operations discussed

Name ____________

Chapter 21, P 7. Basic Cash Budget

Computation of cash receipts from sales on account:

Month	Credit Sales	November	December	January	February	March

1. Cash budget prepared

Tri-State Nurseries, Inc.
Monthly Cash Budgets—Southern Division
For the Quarter Ended March 31, 20x2

	January	February	March	Quarter

2. Loan possibility discussed

Name

Chapter 21, P 8. Budgeted Financial Statements

Preliminary schedules:

Name ______________________

1.	Budgeted income statement prepared

Voyager Video Company, Inc.
Budgeted Income Statement
For the Quarter Ended March 31, 20x1

Name

2.	Budgeted balance sheet prepared

Voyager Video Company, Inc.
Budgeted Balance Sheet
March 31, 20x1

Assets

Liabilities

Stockholders' Equity

Name

Chapter 22, SE 1. Uses of Standard Costs

Chapter 22, SE 2. Purposes of Standard Costs

Standard costs provide the following advantages to management:

1.
2.
3.
4.
5.
6.

Chapter 22, SE 3. Standard Unit Cost Computation

Chapter 22, SE 4. Cost Variance Analysis

SE 4 (concluded)

Possible causes of variances:

Chapter 22, SE 5. Direct Materials Variances

Direct materials price variance	=
	=
	=
Direct materials quantity variance	=
	=
	=

Chapter 22, SE 6. Direct Labor Variances

Direct labor rate variance	=
	=
	=
	=
Direct labor efficiency variance	=
	=
	=
	=

Name

Chapter 22, SE 7. Flexible Budget Preparation

	Levels of Activity Expressed in Units			Variable Cost
Cost Category:	10,000	12,000	14,000	per Unit

Chapter 22, SE 8. Manufacturing Overhead Variances

Controllable manufacturing overhead variance:

Manufacturing overhead volume variance:

Name

Chapter 22, SE 9. Evaluating Managerial Performance

Chapter 22, E 1. Uses of Standard Costs

Chapter 22, E 2. Development of Standard Costs

Computation of new direct materials standards:

Computation of new direct labor standards:

Direct labor rate standards

Machine H:

Machine K:

Chapter 22, E 3. Standard Unit Cost Computation

Name

Chapter 22, E 4. Direct Materials Price and Quantity Variances

Computation of direct materials price variance:

Computation of direct materials quantity variance:

Name

Chapter 22, E 5. Direct Labor Rate and Efficiency Variances

1. Direct labor rate variance computed

2. Direct labor efficiency variance computed

Chapter 22, E 6. Flexible Budget Preparation

Bernard Company Flexible Budget For the Year Ended December 31, 20xx				
	Levels of Activity Expressed in Units			Variable Cost
Cost Category:	18,000	20,000	22,000	per Unit

Name

Chapter 22, E 7. Manufacturing Overhead Variances

Check:		
	Controllable manufacturing overhead variance	
	Manufacturing overhead volume variance	
	Total manufacturing overhead variance	

Chapter 22, E 8. Manufacturing Overhead Variances

1. Under- or overapplied manufacturing overhead for December computed

2. Manufacturing overhead variances computed

Controllable manufacturing overhead variance

Manufacturing overhead volume variance

Check:	
	Controllable manufacturing overhead variance
	Manufacturing overhead volume variance
	Total manufacturing overhead variance

Chapter 22, E 9. Overhead Variance Analysis in an ABC System

1. Under- or overapplied overhead determined

2. Overhead variances computed

Controllable setup overhead variance:

Setup overhead volume variance:

Check:	Controllable setup overhead variance	
	Setup overhead volume variance	
	Total setup overhead cost variance	

Chapter 22, E 10. Evaluating Managerial Performance

Form is not provided; student should use his/her own paper.

Name

Chapter 22, P 1. Developing and Using Standard Costs

1. Total standard cost of direct materials for 20x1 computed
2. Total standard unit cost for 20x1 computed

3. Total standard unit cost for 20x2 computed

Name

Chapter 22, P 2. Direct Materials and Direct Labor Variances

1.	Direct materials price and quantity variances computed

Direct materials price variance:

	Direct Materials	
	Metal (pounds)	Wood (ounces)

Direct materials price variance =

Metal

Wood

Direct materials quantity variance:

	Direct Materials	
	Metal (pounds)	Wood (ounces)

Direct materials quantity variance =

Metal

Wood

Name

1 (concluded)

Check:

2.	Direct labor rate and efficiency variances computed

Direct labor rate variance:

	Direct Labor	
		Trimming/
	Molding	Finishing

Direct labor rate variance =

Molding Department

Trimming/Finishing Department

Direct labor efficiency variance:

	Direct Labor	
		Trimming/
	Molding	Finishing

Direct labor efficiency variance =

Molding Department

Trimming/Finishing Department

Name

2 (concluded)

Check:

Chapter 22, P 3. Flexible Budget and Performance Evaluation

1. Flexible budget prepared

Marwick Home Products Company Cottonwood Division Monthly Flexible Budget				
	Units Produced			Variable
Cost Category:	45,000	50,000	55,000	Cost per Unit

2. Flexible budget formula developed

Flexible budget formula =

Name

3. Revised performance report prepared

Marwick Home Products Company
Cottonwood Division
Performance Report
For April 20xx

Cost Category	46,560 Units Produced		
	Budget	Actual Costs	Variance

4. Performance reports compared

Chapter 22, P 4. Direct Materials, Direct Labor, and Manufacturing Overhead Variances

1. Variances computed

a. Direct materials price variances

Chemicals

Packages

1 (continued)

b. Direct materials quantity variances

Chemicals

Packages

Check:

1 (continued)

c. Direct labor rate variance

d. Direct labor efficiency variance

Check:

e. Controllable manufacturing overhead variance

Name

1 (concluded)

f. **Manufacturing overhead volume variance**

Check:

Name

2. Performance report prepared

Gregor Laboratories, Inc.
Production Performance and Cost Variance Report
Product: Cold-Gone
For the First Week of April, 20x3

Productivity Summary

Normal capacity

Good units produced

Cost and Variance Analysis

	Standard Cost	Actual Cost Incurred	Total Variance	Variance Breakdown	
				Amount	Type

Name

2 (concluded)

Possible Causes of Variances

Chapter 22, P 5. Variance Review: Missing Information

Unknown amounts computed

a.	Total manufacturing overhead variance

b.	Total manufacturing overhead costs applied

c.	Total manufacturing overhead rate per machine hour

Name

d.	Standard fixed manufacturing overhead rate

e.	Normal capacity in machine hours

f.	Actual variable and fixed manufacturing overhead

Chapter 22, P 6. Development of Standards: Direct Materials

1. Total standard direct materials cost per unit determined

2. Standard direct materials unit cost revised based on guaranteed purchase

3. Standard direct materials unit cost revised based on use of substandard spring assemblies

Name ____________________

Chapter 22, P 7. Direct Materials and Direct Labor Variances

1. Direct materials price and quantity variances computed

	Liquid Plastic	Additive
Standard cost		
Less actual cost		
Direct materials price variances		

Direct materials price variance—liquid plastic

Direct materials price variance—additive

Name

1 (concluded)

	Liquid Plastic	Additive
Direct materials quantity variances		

Direct materials quantity variance—liquid plastic

Direct materials quantity variance—additive

	Liquid Plastic	Additive
Check:		
Direct materials price variance		
Direct materials quantity variance		
Total direct materials cost variance		

Name

2.	Direct labor rate and efficiency variances computed

	Molding	Trimming/ Packing
Standard cost		

	Molding	Trimming/ Packing
Direct labor rate variance		

Direct labor rate variance—Molding

Direct labor rate variance—Trimming/Packing

2 (concluded)

	Molding	Trimming/ Packing
Direct labor efficiency variances		

Direct labor efficiency variance—Molding

Direct labor efficiency variance—Trimming/Packing

	Molding	Trimming/ Packing
Check:		
Rate variance		
Efficiency variance		
Total direct labor cost variance		

Name

Chapter 22, P 8. Direct Materials, Direct Labor, and Manufacturing Overhead Variances

Total direct materials variance computed

Standard direct materials cost

1. Direct materials price variance computed

2. Direct materials quantity variance computed

Check:

Direct materials price variance	
Direct materials quantity variance	
Total direct materials cost variance	

2 (concluded)

Total direct labor variance computed

Standard direct labor cost

3. **Direct labor rate variance computed**

4. **Direct labor efficiency variance computed**

Check:

Direct labor rate variance	
Direct labor efficiency variance	
Total direct labor cost variance	

4 (concluded)

Total manufacturing overhead variance computed

Standard manufacturing overhead costs applied to good units produced

5. Controllable manufacturing overhead variance computed

Budgeted manufacturing overhead (flexible budget)

6. Manufacturing overhead volume variance computed

Check:

Controllable manufacturing overhead variance	
Manufacturing overhead volume variance	
Total manufacturing overhead cost variance	

Name

Chapter 23, SE 1. Qualitative and Quantitative Information in Short-Run Decision Analysis

1.
2.
3.
4.
5.

Chapter 23, SE 2. Using Incremental Analysis

Forlands Corporation
Incremental Analysis

	Harvey Machine	Vogle Machine	Difference in Favor of ______ Machine

Chapter 23, SE 3. Make-or-Buy Decision

Zorich Company
Make-or-Buy Decision
Incremental Analysis

	Make Part 23X	Buy Part 23X	Difference in Favor of ______

Decision:

Chapter 23, SE 4. Special Order Decision

Decision:

Name

Chapter 23, SE 5. Decision to Eliminate Unprofitable Segment

Perez Company Segment Profitability Decision			
	West Division	East Division	Total Company

Decision:

Chapter 23, SE 6. Product Mix Decision with Resource Constraints

Let It Snow, Inc. Product Mix Decision			
	Wood	Plastic	Graphite

Order of production:

Chapter 23, SE 7. Sell or Process-Further Decision

Matsuki Industries
Sell or Process-Further Decision

Decision:

Chapter 23, SE 8. Dropping a Segment in a Service Organization

Dental Associates, Inc.
Outsourcing Decision

Costs per Cleaning	Continue to Perform Dental Cleanings	Outsource Dental Cleanings	Difference in Favor of ______ ______ Dental Cleanings

Decision:

Name

Chapter 23, E 1. Relevant Data and Incremental Analysis

1. Relevant data identified

2. Analysis prepared

Socorro Industries
Purchase Decision
Incremental Analysis

	Model A	Model B	Difference in Favor of ______

Decision:

Chapter 23, E 2. Make-or-Buy Decision

Burns Audio Systems, Inc.
Make-or-Buy Decision
Incremental Analysis

	Make	Buy	Difference in Favor of ______

Decision:

Name

Chapter 23, E 3. Special Order Decision

Littell Antiquities, Ltd.
Special Order Decision

Decision:

Chapter 23, E 4. Elimination of Unprofitable Segment

1. Effect of dropped division analyzed

Skylar Glass, Inc.
Segment Profitability Decision

	With Payo Division	Without Payo Division	Difference in Favor of ______ Payo Division

Discussion:

2. Effect of dropped division and reduced sales analyzed

Skylar Glass, Inc.
Segment Profitability Decision

	With Payo Division	Without Payo Division	Difference in Favor of Keeping Payo Division

Discussion:

Name

Chapter 23, E 5. Scarce-Resource Usage

1. Quantities to be produced computed

Brunner, Inc.
Product Mix Decision

	Product A	Product M

Discussion:

2. Income statement prepared

Brunner, Inc.
Income Statement
For the Year Ended December 31, 20x2

Sales		
Variable Costs		
Contribution Margin		

Chapter 23, E 6. Sell or Process-Further Decision

The Meat Market
Product Mix Decision

	Ham	Turkey

Discussion:

Chapter 23, E 7. Special Order for a Service Organization

Discussion:

Name

Chapter 23, P 1. Make-or-Buy Decision

1. Incremental analysis prepared

Westwinds Furniture Company
Make-or-Buy Decision
Incremental Analysis

	Make	Buy	Difference in Favor of ________

2. Unit costs computed

To make

To buy

Check:

Name

Chapter 23, P 2. Special Order Decision

1. Decision analysis prepared

Decision:

2. Lowest price determined

Name ______________________

Chapter 23, P 3. Decision to Eliminate an Unprofitable Product

1. Performance of five existing books analyzed

Singer & Lubbock Publishing Company
Partial Segmented Income Statement
For the Year Ended December 31, 20x2

	Rico	Thompson	Halpern	Nieto	Yardley	Company Totals

2. Comment on the elimination of present books produced

Name

P 3 (concluded)

3. **Replacement books identified**

	Books		
	Book P	Book Q	Book R

Discussion:

Name

Chapter 23, P 4. Product Mix Analysis

1. Machine hours to produce one unit of each product computed

Product	Total Machine Hours		Units Produced		Hours per Unit	
WR1	75,000	hours	30,000	units		hours per unit
WR2	100,000	hours	50,000	units		hours per unit
WR3	20,000	hours	20,000	units		hour per unit
WR4	45,000	hours	90,000	units		hour per unit

2. Contribution margin per machine hour determined

Salagi Machine Tool, Inc.
Product Mix Decision

	Products			
	WR1	WR2	WR3	WR4
Contribution margin per machine hour				

3. Decisions on product lines made

Name

Chapter 23, P 5. Service Mix Decision

1. Best service mix determined

Dr. Robert Domingo Service Mix Decision	Office Visits	Phone Calls	Weight Loss Support Group

2. Service mix and contribution margin identified

Discussion:

Name

P 5 (concluded)

3. **Revised service mix and contribution margin identified**

4. **Decision recommended and explained**

Name ______________________

Chapter 23, P 6. Sell or Process-Further Decision

1. Relevant costs and revenues identified

	Relevant Revenue	Relevant Costs	Net Profit

2. Expansion discussed

3. Incremental analysis performed

Bagels, Inc.
Sell or Process-Further Decision

	Bagels with Cream Cheese	Bagel Sandwiches

Name ______________________

Chapter 23, P 7. Segment Profitability Decision

1. Impact of dropping Baseball line analyzed

AllSports, Inc., Bristol Branch
Segment Profitability Decision
(Amounts in Thousands)

	With Baseball	Without Baseball	Difference in Favor of ________ Baseball
Sales			
Less variable costs			
Contribution margin			
Less direct fixed costs			
Segment margin			
Less common fixed costs			
Net income (loss)			

Result:

P 7 (continued)

2. Impact of adding In-Line Skating line analyzed

AllSports, Inc., Bristol Branch
Projected Segmented Income Statement
(Amounts in Thousands)

	Football	Baseball	Basketball	In-Line Skating	Bristol Branch
Sales					
Less variable costs					
Contribution margin					
Less direct fixed costs					
Segment margin					
Less common fixed costs					
Net income					

AllSports, Inc., Bristol Branch
Segment Profitability Decision
(Amounts in Thousands)

	Without In-Line Skating	With In-Line Skating	Difference in Favor of Adding In-Line Skating
Sales			
Less variable costs			
Contribution margin			
Less direct fixed costs			
Segment margin			
Less common fixed costs			
Net income			

Result:

Name

P 7 (concluded)

3. **Decreases in sales analyzed**

AllSports, Inc., Bristol Branch
Segmented Income Statement
For the Year Ended Deember 31, 20x0
(Amounts in Thousands)

	Football	Baseball	Basketball	In-Line Skating	Bristol Branch
Sales					
Less variable costs					
Contribution margin					
Less direct fixed costs					
Segment margin					
Less common fixed costs					
Net income					

AllSports, Inc., Bristol Branch
Segment Profitability Decision
(Amounts in Thousands)

	Keep Baseball Line	Add In-Line Skating Line and Drop Baseball Line	Difference in Favor of Adding In-Line Skating and Dropping Baseball
Sales			
Less variable costs			
Contribution margin			
Less direct fixed costs			
Segment margin			
Less common fixed costs			
Net income			

4. **Decision recommended with explanation**

Name

Chapter 23, P 8. Special Order Decision

1. Decision analysis prepared

Net income from special order

Decision:

2. Lowest price determined

Name

Chapter 24, SE 1. Manager's Role in Capital Investment Decisions

Form is not provided; student should use his/her own paper.

Chapter 24, SE 2. Minimum Desired Rate of Return

Computation of average cost of capital:

Amount	Proportion of Capital Mix	x	Cost	=	Weighted Cost		
						=	

Chapter 24, SE 3. Capital Budgeting Cost and Revenue Measures

Form is not provided; student should use his/her own paper.

Chapter 24, SE 4. Capital Investment Decision: Payback Period Method

Chapter 24, SE 5. Time Value of Money

Form is not provided; student should use his/her own paper.

Name

Chapter 24, SE 6. Capital Investment Decision: Net Present Value Method

Chapter 24, SE 7. Salvage Value and the Net Present Value Method

The present value of the salvage value is:

Chapter 24, E 1. Capital Investment Decision Cycle

1 and 2. Form is not provided; student should use his/her own paper.

Chapter 24, E 2. Minimum Desired Rate of Return

Source of Capital	Cost	x	Proportion of Capital Mix	=	Weighted Cost
Debt financing					
Preferred stock					
Common stock					
Retained earnings					
Weighted average cost of capital					=

Name

Chapter 24, E 3. Analysis of Relevant Information

1. Relevant costs and revenues identified

2. Cash-flow analysis prepared

	Model One	Model Two	Difference
Net cash flow difference			

Discussion:

Name

Chapter 24, E 4. Capital Investment Decision: Accounting Rate-of-Return Method

Decision:

Chapter 24, E 5. Capital Investment Decision: Payback Period Method

Decision:

Name

Chapter 24, E 6. Using Present Value Tables

1.

2.

3.

4.

5.

Year	1	$35,000	x	=	
	2	20,000	x	=	
	3	30,000	x	=	
	4	40,000	x	=	
	5	50,000	x	=	
Total					

6.

Chapter 24, E 7. Present Value Computations

1. Net present value of each alternative computed

Machine K

Year	Net Cash Inflow	12% Multiplier	Present Value
1	12000 —		
2	12000 —		
3	14000 —		
4	19000 —		
5	20000 —		
6	22000 —		
7	23000 —		
8	24000 —		
9	25000 —		
10	20000 —		
Salvage	14000 —		
Net present value			

Machine L

	Net Cash Inflow	12% Multiplier	Present Value
Present value of ten equal			
amounts of $17,500 each	17500 —		
Salvage	12000 —		
Net present value			

2. Purchase recommended

Name

Chapter 24, E 8. Capital Investment Decision: Net Present Value Method

Year	Net Cash Inflow	x	14% Multiplier	=	Present Value
1					
2					
3					
4					
5					
6					
Total present value					
Less purchase price of machine					

Decision:

Chapter 24, P 1. Minimum Desired Rate of Return

1. Weighted average cost of capital for the current year computed

Source of Capital	Cost	x	Proportion of Capital Mix	=	Weighted Cost		
Debt financing							
Preferred stock							
Common stock							
Retained earnings							
Weighted average							
cost of capital						=	

2. Proposed capital investments identified

The projects that should be implemented are:

Name

Chapter 24, P 2. Accounting Rate-of-Return and Payback Period Methods

1. Net income computed

Blue Island Corporation
Analysis of Capital Investments
Projected Annual Net Income

	Coupe Machine	Metro Machine

P 2 (continued)

2. Accounting rate of return computed

Accounting Rate of Return	=	
Coupe Machine	=	
	=	
Metro Machine	=	
	=	

P 2 (concluded)

3. Payback period computed

Payback Period	=	
Coupe Machine	=	
Metro Machine	=	

4. Recommendation made

Decision criteria:

	Coupe Machine		Metro Machine	
Accounting rate of return				
Payback period		years		years

Discussion:

Chapter 24, P 3. Even Versus Uneven Cash Flows

1. Net present value of Jenny's cash flows computed

Year	Net Cash Inflow	10% Multiplier	Present Value

2. Net present value of purchasing Sean computed

Year	Net Cash Inflow	10% Multiplier	Present Value

3. Recommendation made

Name

Chapter 24, P 4. Net Present Value Method

1. Net present value method applied to capital investment decision

2. Decision about purchase of machine based on a 14% desired rate of return

Present value of net cash inflows

Recommendation:

Chapter 24, P 5. Capital Investment Decision: Comprehensive

1. Analysis prepared

Cash flow analysis:

Year	Cash Inflows	Cash Outflows	Net Cash Inflow
1	$ 325,000	$ 250,000	
2	320,000	250,000	
3	315,000	250,000	
4	310,000	250,000	
Totals			

1a. Accounting rate-of-return method

	Increase in Net Income				
Year	Net Cash Inflow	–	Depreciation	=	Net Income
1					
2					
3					
4					
Totals					

Accounting Rate of Return	=	
	=	
	=	

Name

P 5 (concluded)

1b. Payback method

Payback period is __________ years.

1c. Net present value method (minimum desired rate of return = 12%)

Year	Net Cash Inflow	x	12% Multipliers	=	Present Value
1					
2					
3					
4					
4	(salvage)				
Total present value					
Less: Cost of initial investment					

2. Summary and recommendation

Name

Chapter 24, P 6. Accounting Rate-of-Return and Payback Period Methods

1. Net income computed

Coghill Company Analysis of Capital Investments Projected Annual Net Income		
	Darcy Machine	Kypros Machine

Name

P 6 (continued)	
2.	**Accounting rate of return computed**

Accounting Rate of Return	**=**	
Darcy Machine	**=**	
	=	
Kypros Machine	**=**	
	=	

P 6 (concluded)

3. Payback period computed

Payback Period	=	
Darcy Machine	=	
Kypros Machine	=	

4. Recommendation made

Decision criteria:

	Darcy Machine		Kypros Machine	
Accounting rate of return		%		%
Payback period		years		years

Name

Chapter 24, P 7. Net Present Value Method

1. Net present value of the old building's cash flows computed

Year		Net Cash Inflow	14% Multiplier	Present Value
Net present value				

2. Net present value if new building is purchased

Year		Net Cash Inflow	14% Multiplier	Present Value

3. Recommendation made

Name

Chapter 24, P 8. Net Present Value Method

1. Decision about purchase of machine based on a 14 percent desired rate of return

Present value of net cash inflows

Recommendation:

2. Decision about purchase of machine based on a 16 percent desired rate of return

Present value of net cash inflows

Recommendation:

Name

Chapter 25, SE 1. Rules for Establishing Prices

Form is not provided; student should his/her own paper.

Chapter 25, SE 2. Traditional Economic Pricing Concept

Form is not provided; student should his/her own paper.

Chapter 25, SE 3. External Factors that Influence Prices

External market factors such as the following must also be considered:
(Form is not provided; student should his/her own paper.)

Chapter 25, SE 4. Cost-Based Price Setting

Markup Percentage	=	
	=	
	=	
Gross-Margin-Based Price	=	
	=	

Chapter 25, SE 5. Pricing a Service

Total billing price:

Chapter 25, SE 6. Committed Costs and Target Costing
Form is not provided; student should use his/her own paper.
Chapter 25, SE 7. Pricing Using Target Costing
Form is not provided; student should use his/her own paper.
Chapter 25, SE 8. Decision to Use Transfer Prices
Form is not provided; student should use his/her own paper.
Chapter 25, SE 9. Cost-Based Versus Market-Based Transfer Prices
Form is not provided; student should use his/her own paper.
Chapter 25, SE 10. Developing a Negotiated Transfer Price
Form is not provided; student should use his/her own paper.
Chapter 25, E 1. Pricing Policy Objectives
Form is not provided; student should use his/her own paper.

Name

Chapter 25, E 2. Traditional Economic Pricing Theory

1.	Graph of total revenue and total cost curves drawn

2.	Estimated selling price calculated

Chapter 25, E 3. External and Internal Pricing Factors

1. Unit selling prices computed

	Gripper		Roadster	
	One tire	Four tires	One tire	Four tires

2. Influence of cost on sales price discussed

3. Other pricing factors identified

Other pricing considerations include:

Chapter 25, E 4. Price Determination

1. Unit cost computed

Cost Categories	Total Projected Costs

2. Markup percentage and unit selling price computed, using the gross margin pricing method

Markup Percentage	=	
	=	
Gross-Margin-Based Price	=	
	=	

Chapter 25, E 5. Pricing a Service

1. Projected cost computed

Cost Categories	Total Projected Costs

2. Inspection charge, using the gross margin pricing method, determined

Markup Percentage	=	
	=	
Gross-Margin-Based Price	=	
	=	

E 5 (concluded)		
3.	**Inspection charge, using the return on assets pricing method, computed**	
Return-on-Assets-Based Price	=	
Desired Rate of Return	=	
Return-on-Assets-Based Price	=	

Name

Chapter 25, E 6. Time and Materials Pricing

The price quoted should be computed as follows:

	Cost	Overhead Markup	Total Cost
Materials			
Labor			
Total cost			
Profit markup			
Total price for job			

Chapter 25, E 7. Target Costing and Pricing

Target cost computed:

Target cost:

Projected unit cost of the product calculated:

Decision:

Name

Chapter 25, E 8. Target Costing

1. Target cost computed

Target cost =

2. Projected unit cost of AutoDrill computed

3. Production decision discussed

Production decision calculations:

Name

Chapter 25, E 9. Transfer Price Comparison

1. Cost-plus transfer price developed

Cost Categories	Cost per Unit

2. Transfer price discussed

Name

Chapter 25, P 1. Pricing Decision

Before computing the various selling prices, the cost analysis must be completed and restructured to supply the information needed for the pricing computations.

Cost Categories	Unit Cost	Total Projected Costs

P 1 (concluded)

1. **Selling price, using the gross margin pricing method, computed**

Markup Percentage =

=

Gross-Margin-Based Price =

=

2. **Selling price recommended**

Sales Level	Unit Price	Unit Cost*	Unit Profit	Total Profit
600,000				
540,000				
480,000				

Recommendation:

3. **Selling price reevaluated**

Name

Chapter 25, P 2. Cost-Based Pricing

Before computing the various selling prices, the cost analysis must be completed and restructured to supply the information needed for the pricing computations.

Cost Categories	Total Projected Costs	Regular Blend	Mint Blend	Choco Blend

P 2 (concluded)

1. Selling prices, using the gross margin pricing method, computed

Markup Percentage	=	
Gross-Margin-Based Price	=	

Regular Blend:

Markup Percentage	=	
Gross-Margin-Based Price	=	
	=	

Mint Blend:

Markup Percentage	=	
Gross-Margin-Based Price	=	
	=	

Choco Blend:

Markup Percentage	=	
Gross-Margin-Based Price	=	
	=	

2. Competition's influence on price discussed

Form is not provided; student should use his/her own paper.

Name

Chapter 25, P 3. Time and Materials Pricing			
1.	Markup percentages computed		
	Markup Percentage	=	
a.	Direct materials and supplies	=	
		=	
b.	Direct labor	=	
		=	
2.	Billing prepared		

Materials		
	2" x 4" x 8' cedar	
	2" x 6" x 8' cedar	
	2" x 8" x 8' cedar	
	4" x 8' sheets, 1/2" plywood	
	Framed windows	
	Framed doors	
	4" x 8' sheets, siding	
	Supplies	
	Total direct materials and supplies	
Materials overhead		
Direct labor		
	Laborers/helpers	
	Semiskilled carpenters	
	Carpenters	
	Total direct labor cost	
Direct labor overhead		
Total billing		

Name

Chapter 25, P 4. Pricing Using Target Costing

1.	Target costs computed

Speed-Calc 4:	
Speed-Calc 5:	

2.	Projected unit cost determined

	Speed-Calc 4	Speed-Calc 5
Raw materials cost		
Computer chip cost		
Total raw materials and parts cost		
Production labor		
Speed-Calc 4		
Speed-Calc 5		
Assembly labor		
Speed-Calc 4		
Speed-Calc 5		
Activity-based costs		
Materials/parts handling activity		
Speed-Calc 4		
Speed-Calc 5		
Production activity		
Speed-Calc 4		
Speed-Calc 5		
Marketing/delivery activity		
Speed-Calc 4		
Speed-Calc 5		
Projected total unit cost		

Name

P 4 (concluded)

3.	**Production decision discussed**

	Speed-Calc 4	**Speed-Calc 5**

Chapter 25, P 5. Developing Transfer Prices

1. Transfer price recommended

Cost Categories	Cost per Unit

2. Transfer price reevaluated

Name ______________________

Chapter 25, P 6. Pricing Decision

Before computing the various selling prices, the cost analysis must be completed and restructured to supply the information needed for pricing computations.

Cost Categories	Unit Cost	Total Projected Costs

Name

P 6 (concluded)

1. **Selling price, using the gross margin pricing method, computed**

Markup Percentage	=	
	=	
Gross-Margin-Based Price	=	
	=	
	=	

2. **Selling price recommended**

Sales Level	Unit Price	Unit Cost	Unit Profit	Total Profit

3. **Selling price reevaluated**

Name

Chapter 25, P 7. Pricing Using Target Costing

1. Target cost computed

Product Y14:

Product Z33:

2. Projected unit costs of products determined

	Product Y14	Product Z33
Raw materials cost		
Purchased parts cost		
Total raw materials and parts cost		
Manufacturing labor		
Y14		
Z33		
Assembly labor		
Y14		
Z33		
Activity-based costs		
Materials handling activity		
Y14		
Z33		
Production activity		
Y14		
Z33		
Product delivery activity		
Y14		
Z33		
Projected total unit cost		

P 7 (concluded)

3. Production decision discussed

	Product Y14	Product Z33

Name

Chapter 25, P 8. Developing Transfer Prices

1. Cost computed

Cost Categories	Budgeted Total Costs	Cost per Unit (400,000 units)

2. Transfer price recommended and discussed

Form is not provided; student should use his/her own paper.

Name ______________________

Chapter 26, SE 1. Traits of a Cost Management System

Form is not provided; student should use his/her own paper.

Chapter 26, SE 2. Continuous Improvement

Form is not provided; student should use his/her own paper.

Chapter 26, SE 3. Cost of Quality in a Service Business

Policy processing improvements:

Customer complaints response:

Policy writer training:

Policy error losses:

Policy proofing:

Chapter 26, SE 4. Measures of Quality

Costs of Conformance	=	
	=	
Costs of Nonconformance	=	
	=	

a.	Total Costs of Quality as a Percentage of Sales	=	
b.	Ratio of Costs of Conformance to Total Costs of Quality	=	
c.	Ratio of Costs of Nonconformance to Total Costs of Quality	=	
d.	Costs of Nonconformance as a Percentage of Total Sales	=	

Name

Chapter 26, SE 5. Nonfinancial Measures of Quality

Nonfinancial measures of good quality:

Nonfinancial measures of poor quality:

Chapter 26, SE 6. Total Product Delivery Performance Evaluation

Week	Purchase Order Lead Time		Production Cycle Time		Delivery Time		Total Delivery Cycle Time	
1	2.4	days	3.5	days	4.0	days		days
2	2.3	days	3.5	days	3.5	days		days
3	2.4	days	3.3	days	3.4	days		days
4	2.5	days	3.2	days	3.3	days		days

Evaluation:

Chapter 26, SE 7. Full Cost Profit Margin

	July–September		October–December	
	Amount	%	Amount	%

Evaluation:

Name

Chapter 26, E 1. Adapting to Changing Information Needs

Form is not provided; student should use his/her own paper.

Chapter 26, E 2. Costs of Quality

1.

Konstantinos Corp.
Analysis of Costs of Quality
For the Month Ended January 31, 20xx

2. (Form is not provided; student should use his/her own paper.)

Name

Chapter 26, E 3. Measuring Costs of Quality

	Dept. A	Dept. B	Totals
Annual Sales	$9,200,000	$11,000,000	$20,200,000

Discussion:

Chapter 26, E 4. Nonfinancial Measures of Quality and TQM

Form is not provided; student should use his/her own paper.

Chapter 26, E 5. Nonfinancial Data Analysis

	Weeks				Weekly
	1	2	3	4	Average

Analysis:

Name ______________________

Chapter 26, E 6. Full Cost Profit Margin

Information after installing new system and adopting full cost profit margin recast:

	Product AJ–25
Average monthly revenue	1350000 —

Full cost profit margin calculation:

Full cost profit margin as a percentage of revenue	
Operating profit as a percentage of revenue	

Chapter 26, E 7. Margin and Performance Measurement

The following percentages of total sales were computed for the data given:

	Product Line 1	Product Line 2	Product Line 3	Product Line 4	Company Totals*
Total sales					
Contribution margin					
Full cost profit margin					
Total nontraceable costs					
Net income					

Discussion:

Chapter 26, P 1. Costs and Nonfinancial Measures of Quality

1 and 2. Costs of quality and category percentages of sales computed

	East Division		Central Division		West Division	
	Amount	% of Sales	Amount	% of Sales	Amount	% of Sales
Annual sales	8500000 —		9500000 —		13000000 —	

P 1 (concluded)

3. Cost-of-quality data analyzed

4. Nonfinancial measures of quality analyzed

Name ______________________

Chapter 26, P 2. Interpreting Measures of Quality	
1.	Divisions ranked (highest to lowest) by quality effort and results
2.	Key measures identified (three of the following)
3.	
4.	
Form is not provided; student should use his/her own paper.	

Name

Chapter 26, P 3. Analysis of Nonfinancial Data

The data given were reorganized in the following manner and three additional pieces of information not required by the problem—delivery cycle time, waste time, and estimated number of units sold—were calculated from the given information for illustrative purposes.

1. Department performance analyzed

	Weeks								Weekly
	1	2	3	4	5	6	7	8	Average
Product quality performance									
Total product delivery performance									
Inventory control performance									
Materials cost and scrap control									
performance									
Machine management performance									

Name

P 3 (concluded)

2. Report to department superintendent prepared

Chapter 26, P 4. Full Cost Profit Margin

1. Information recast into before and after new system installed and full cost profit margin adopted

	Assembly B4	Assembly C10	Assembly F17
Total revenue	4700000 —	5250000 —	3500000 —

P 4 (concluded)

2. **Full cost profit margin and contribution margin contrasted**

Form is not provided; student should use his/her own paper.

3. **Product performance before installing new system and adopting full cost profit margin evaluated**

	Assembly B4	Assembly C10	Assembly F17

4. **Product performance after installing new system and adopting full cost profit margin evaluated**

	Assembly B4	Assembly C10	Assembly F17

5. **Product C10 analyzed**

Form is not provided; student should use his/her own paper.

Name ______________________

Chapter 26, P 5. Costs and Nonfinancial Measures of Quality

1 and 2. Costs of quality and category percentages of sales computed

	Currence Company		Aspen Company		Prescott Company	
	Amount	% of Sales	Amount	% of Sales	Amount	% of Sales
Annual sales	11,600,000 —		13,300,000 —		10,800,000 —	

3. Cost-of-quality data interpreted

4. Nonfinancial measures of quality analyzed

Form is not provided; student should use his/her own paper.

Name ____________________

Chapter 26, P 6. Analysis of Nonfinancial Data

The data given were reorganized in the following manner, and three additional pieces of information not reuqired by the problem—delivery cycle time, waste time, and estimated number of units sold—were calculated from the given information for illustrative purposes.

1. Machine line performance analyzed

	Weeks								Weekly
	1	2	3	4	5	6	7	8	Average
Product quality performance									
Total product delivery performance									
Inventory control performance									
Materials cost and scrap control performance									
Machine management performance									

P 6 (concluded)

2. **Report to management prepared**

Name

Chapter 27, SE 1. Objectives and Standards of Financial Statement Analysis

1.
2.
3.
4.
5.

Chapter 27, SE 2. Sources of Information

1.
2.
3.
4.
5.

Chapter 27, SE 3. Trend Analysis

	2002	2001	2000

Chapter 27, SE 4. Horizontal Analysis

SiteWorks, Inc.
Comparative Income Statements
For the Years Ended December 31, 20x1 and 20x0

	20x1	20x0	Increase or Decrease Amount	Increase or Decrease Percentage
Net Sales	180000 —	145000 —		
Cost of Goods Sold	112000 —	88000 —		
Gross Margin	68000 —	57000 —		
Operating Expenses	40000 —	30000 —		
Operating Income	28000 —	27000 —		
Interest Expense	7000 —	5000 —		
Income Before Income Taxes	21000 —	22000 —		
Income Taxes	7000 —	8000 —		
Net Income	14000 —	14000 —		
Earnings per Share	1 40	1 40		

Name

Chapter 27, SE 5. Vertical Analysis

SiteWorks, Inc. Common-Size Balance Sheets December 31, 20x1 and 20x0		
	20x1	20x0
Assets		
Current Assets		
Property, Plant, and Equipment (net)		
Total Assets		
Liabilities and Stockholders' Equity		
Current Liabilities		
Long-Term Liabilities		
Stockholders' Equity		
Total Liabilities and Stockholders' Equity		

Name

Chapter 27, SE 6. Liquidity Analysis

	20x1	20x0
Current ratio:		
Quick ratio:		
Receivable turnover:		
Average days' sales uncollected:		

(continued)

Name

Chapter 27, SE 6. (continued)

	20x1	20x0
Inventory turnover:		
Average days' inventory on hand:		

Name ______________________

Chapter 27, SE 7. Profitability Analysis

	20x1	20x0
Profit margin:		
Asset turnover:		
Return on assets:		
Return on equity:		

Name

Chapter 27, SE 8. Long-Term Solvency Analysis

	20x1	20x0
Debt to equity ratio:		
Interest coverage ratio:		

Name

Chapter 27, SE 9. Cash Flow Adequacy Analysis

	20x1	20x0
Cash flow yield:		
Cash flows to sales:		
Cash flows to assets:		
Free cash flow:		

Name

Chapter 27, SE 10. Market Strength Analysis

	20x1	20x0
Price/earnings ratio:		
Dividends yield:		

Chapter 27, E 1. Objectives, Standards, and Sources of Information for Financial Statement Analysis

1.	5.
2.	6.
3.	7.
4.	

Chapter 27, E 2. Horizontal Analysis

Lindquist Company
Comparative Balance Sheets
December 31, 20x2 and 20x1

	20x2	20x1	Increase or Decrease Amount	Increase or Decrease Percentage
Assets				
Current Assets	37200 —	25600 —		
Property, Plant, and Equipment (net)	218928 —	194400 —		
Total Assets	256128 —	220000 —		
Liabilities and Stockholders' Equity				
Current Liabilities	22400 —	6400 —		
Long-Term Liabilities	70000 —	80000 —		
Stockholders' Equity	163728 —	133600 —		
Total Liabilities and Stockholders' Equity	256128 —	220000 —		

Comment:

Name ____________________

Chapter 27, E 3. Trend Analysis

	20x5	20x4	20x3	20x2	20x1
Net sales					
Cost of goods sold					
General and administrative expenses					
Operating income					

Comment:

Chapter 27, E 4. Vertical Analysis

Lindquist Company
Common-Size Income Statements
For the Years Ended December 31, 20x2 and 20x1

	20x2	20x1
Net Sales		
Cost of Goods Sold		
Gross Margin		
Selling Expenses		
General Expenses		
Total Operating Expenses		
Net Operating Income		

Comment:

Chapter 27, E 5. Liquidity Analysis

	20x2	20x1
Current ratio		
Quick ratio		
Receivable turnover		
Average days' sales uncollected		
Inventory turnover		
Average days' inventory on hand		

Name

Chapter 27, E 5. (continued)

Comment:

Chapter 27, E 6.

Year	Receivable Turnover	Inventory Turnover
20x1:		
20x2:		
20x3:		
20x4:		

Name ____________________

Chapter 27, E 7. Profitability Analysis

	20x2	20x1
Profit margin		
Asset turnover		
Return on assets		
Return on equity*		

Name

Chapter 27, E 8. Long-Term Solvency and Market Strength Ratios

	Company X	Company Y
Debt to equity ratio		
Interest coverage ratio		
P/E ratio		
Dividends yield		

Chapter 27, E 9. Cash Flow Adequacy Analysis	
Cash flow yield	
Cash flows to sales	
Cash flows to assets	
Free cash flow	

Name

Chapter 27, E 10. Preparation of Statements from Ratios and Incomplete Data

Pandit Corporation
Income Statement
For the Year Ended December 31, 20x1
(in thousands of dollars)

Net Sales		18000 —	
Cost of Goods Sold			(a)
Gross Margin			(b)
Operating Expenses			
Selling Expenses	(c)		
Administrative Expenses	234 —		
Total Operating Expenses			(d)
Income from Operations			(e)
Interest Expense		162 —	
Income Before Income Taxes			(f)
Income Taxes		620 —	
Net Income			(g)

Pandit Corporation
Balance Sheet
December 31, 20x1
(in thousands of dollars)

Assets			
Cash	(h)		
Accounts Receivable (net)	(i)		
Inventories	(j)		
Total Current Assets			(k)
Property, Plant, and Equipment (net)		5400 —	
Total Assets			(l)
Liabilities and Stockholders' Equity			
Current Liabilities	(m)		
Bond Payable, 9% interest	(n)		
Total Liabilities			(o)
Common Stock, $20 par value	3000 —		
Paid-in Capital in Excess of Par Value, Common	2600 —		
Retained Earnings	4000 —		
Total Stockholders' Equity		9600 —	
Total Liabilities and Stockholders' Equity			(p)

Chapter 27, E 10. (concluded)

Computations:

Name

Chapter 27, P 1. Horizontal and Vertical Analysis

1. Schedules showing amount and percentage changes prepared

Mariano Corporation
Comparative Income Statements
For the Years Ended December 31, 20x2 and 20x1
(in thousands of dollars)

			Increase or Decrease	
	20x2	20x1	Amount	Percentage
Net Sales	3,276,800 —	3,146,400 —		
Cost of Goods Sold	2,088,800 —	2,008,400 —		
Gross Margin	1,188,000 —	1,138,000 —		
Operating Expenses				
Selling Expenses	476,800 —	518,000 —		
Administrative Expenses	447,200 —	423,200 —		
Total Operating Expenses	924,000 —	941,200 —		
Income from Operations	264,000 —	196,800 —		
Interest Expense	65,600 —	39,200 —		
Income Before Income Taxes	198,400 —	157,600 —		
Income Taxes	62,400 —	56,800 —		
Net Income	136,000 —	100,800 —		

Name

Mariano Corporation
Comparative Balance Sheets
December 31, 20x2 and 20x1
(in thousands of dollars)

	20x2	20x1	Increase or Decrease Amount	Increase or Decrease Percentage
Assets				
Cash	81,200 —	40,800 —		
Accounts Receivable (net)	235,600 —	229,200 —		
Inventory	574,800 —	594,800 —		
Property, Plant, and Equipment (net)	750,000 —	720,000 —		
Total Assets	1,641,600 —	1,584,800 —		
Liabilities and Stockholders' Equity				
Accounts Payable	267,600 —	477,200 —		
Notes Payable (Short Term)	200,000 —	400,000 —		
Bonds Payable	400,000 —	0 —		
Common Stock, $10 par value	400,000 —	400,000 —		
Retained Earnings	374,000 —	307,600 —		
Total Liabilities and Stockholders' Equity	1,641,600 —	1,584,800 —		

Name

2. Common-size income statements and balance sheet prepared

Mariano Corporation
Common-Size Income Statements
For the Years Ended December 31, 20x2 and 20x1

	20x2	20x1
Net Sales		
Cost of Goods Sold		
Gross Margin		
Operating Expenses		
Selling Expenses		
Administrative Expenses		
Total Operating Expenses		
Income from Operations		
Interest Expense		
Income Before Income Taxes		
Income Taxes		
Net Income		

Mariano Corporation
Common-Size Balance Sheets
December 31, 20x2 and 20x1

	20x2	20x1
Assets		
Cash		
Accounts Receivable (net)		
Inventory		
Property, Plant, and Equipment (net)		
Total Assets		
Liabilities and Stockholders' Equity		
Accounts Payable		
Notes Payable (Short Term)		
Bonds Payable		
Common Stock, $10 par value		
Retained Earnings		
Total Liabilities and Stockholders' Equity		

3.	Results commented on

Name

Chapter 27, P 2. Analyzing the Effects of Transactions on Ratios

	Transaction	Ratio	Effect		
			Increase	Decrease	None
a.	Sold merchandise on account.	Current ratio			
b.	Sold merchandise on account.	Inventory turnover			
c.	Collected on accounts receivable.	Quick ratio			
d.	Wrote off an uncollectible account.	Receivable turnover			
e.	Paid on accounts payable.	Current ratio			
f.	Declared cash dividend.	Return on equity			
g.	Incurred advertising expense.	Profit margin			
h.	Issued stock dividend.	Debt to equity ratio			
i.	Issued bond payable.	Asset turnover			
j.	Accrued interest expense.	Current ratio			
k.	Paid previously declared cash dividend.	Dividends yield			
l.	Purchased treasury stock.	Return on assets			
m.	Recorded depreciation expense.	Cash flow yield			

Name

Chapter 27, P 3. Ratio Analysis

Ratio	20x2	20x1	Favorable (F) or Unfavorable (U) Change
1. Liquidity analysis			
a. Current ratio			
b. Quick ratio			
c. Receivable turnover			
d. Average days' sales uncollected			
e. Inventory turnover			
f. Average days' inventory on hand			

Name ____________

Ratio	20x2	20x1	Favorable (F) or Unfavorable (U) Change
2. Profitability analysis a. Profit margin			
b. Asset turnover			
c. Return on assets			
d. Return on equity			
3. Long-term solvency analysis a. Debt to equity ratio			
b. Interest coverage ratio			

Name ____________________

Ratio	20x2	20x1	Favorable (F) or Unfavorable (U) Change
4. Cash flow adequacy analysis			
a. Cash flow yield			
b. Cash flows to sales			
c. Cash flows to assets			
d. Free cash flow			
5. Market strength analysis			
a. Price/earnings ratio			
b. Dividends yield			

Name ____________________

Chapter 27, P 4. Comprehensive Ratio Analysis of Two Companies

Ratio	Allison Corporation	Marker Corporation
1. Liquidity analysis		
a. Current ratio		
b. Quick ratio		
c. Receivable turnover		
d. Average days' sales uncollected		
e. Inventory turnover		
f. Average days' inventory on hand		

(continued)

Name

1 (concluded)

Ratio	Allison Corporation	Marker Corporation
2. Profitability analysis		
a. Profit margin		
b. Asset turnover		
c. Return on assets		
d. Return on equity		
3. Long-term solvency analysis		
a. Debt to equity ratio		
b. Interest coverage ratio		

(continued)

Name ______________________

Ratio	Allison Corporation	Marker Corporation
4. Cash flow adequacy analysis		
a. Cash flow yield		
b. Cash flows to sales		
c. Cash flows to assets		
d. Free cash flow		
5. Market strength analysis		
a. Price/earnings ratio		
b. Dividends yield		

Name

6.	Comparative analysis			

Ratio Name		Allison Corporation	Marker Corporation	Company with More Favorable Ratio
1.	Liquidity analysis			
a.	Current ratio			
b.	Quick ratio			
c.	Receivable turnover			
d.	Average days' sales uncollected			
e.	Inventory turnover			
f.	Average days inventory on hand			
2.	Profitability analysis			
a.	Profit margin			
b.	Asset turnover			
c.	Return on assets			
d.	Return on equity			
3.	Long-term solvency analysis			
a.	Debt to equity ratio			
b.	Interest coverage ratio			
4.	Cash flow adequacy analysis			
a.	Cash flow yield			
b.	Cash flows to sales			
c.	Cash flows to assets			
d.	Free cash flow			
5.	Market strength analysis			
a.	Price-earnings ratio			
b.	Dividends yield			

7.	Use of information from prior years

Name ______________________

Chapter 27, P 5. Analyzing the Effects of Transactions on Ratios					
			Effect		
Transaction		Ratio	Increase	Decrease	None
a.	Issued common stock for cash.	Asset turnover			
b.	Declared cash dividend.	Current ratio			
c.	Sold treasury stock.	Return on equity			
d.	Borrowed cash by issuing note payable.	Debt to equity ratio			
e.	Paid salaries expense.	Inventory turnover			
f.	Purchased merchandise for cash.	Current ratio			
g.	Sold equipment for cash.	Receivable turnover			
h.	Sold merchandise on account.	Quick ratio			
i.	Paid current portion of long-term debt.	Return on assets			
j.	Gave sales discount.	Profit margin			
k.	Purchased marketable securities for cash.	Quick ratio			
l.	Declared 5% stock dividend.	Current ratio			
m.	Purchased a building.	Free cash flow			

Name

Chapter 27, P 6. Ratio Analysis

Ratio	20x6	20x5	Change*
1. Liquidity analysis			
a. Current ratio			
b. Quick ratio			
c. Receivable turnover			
d. Average days' sales uncollected			
e. Inventory turnover			
f. Average days' inventory on hand			

*Favorable change: F; unfavorable change: U.

Ratio	20x6	20x5	Change*
2. Profitability analysis			
a. Profit margin			
b. Asset turnover			
c. Return on assets			
d. Return on equity			
3. Long-term solvency analysis			
a. Debt to equity ratio			
b. Interest coverage ratio			

*Favorable change: F; unfavorable change: U.

Name ____________

Ratio	20x6	20x5	Change*
4. Cash flow adequacy analysis			
a. Cash flow yield			
b. Cash flows to sales			
c. Cash flows to assets			
d. Free cash flow			
5. Market strength analysis			
a. Price/earnings ratio			
b. Dividends yield			

*Favorable change: F; unfavorable change: U.

Name

Chapter 27, P 7. Comprehensive Ratio Analysis of Two Companies

Ratio	Emax	Savlow
1. Liquidity analysis		
a. Current ratio		
b. Quick ratio		
c. Receivable turnover		
d. Average days' sales uncollected		
e. Inventory turnover		
f. Average days' inventory on hand		

(continued)

Name

Ratio	Emax	Savlow
2. Profitability analysis		
a. Profit margin		
b. Asset turnover		
c. Return on assets		
d. Return on equity		
3. Long-term solvency analysis		
a. Debt to equity ratio		
b. Interest coverage ratio		

(continued)

Name

Ratio	Emax	Savlow
4. Cash flow adequacy analysis		
a. Cash flow yield		
b. Cash flows to sales		
c. Cash flows to assets		
d. Free cash flow		
5. Market strength analysis		
a. Price/earnings ratio		
b. Dividends yield		

6.	Comparative analysis			

		Emax	Savlow	Company with More Favorable Ratio
Ratio Name				
1.	Liquidity analysis			
	a. Current ratio			
	b. Quick ratio			
	c. Receivable turnover			
	d. Average days' sales uncollected			
	e. Inventory turnover			
	f. Average days' inventory on hand			
2.	Profitability analysis			
	a. Profit margin			
	b. Asset turnover			
	c. Return on assets			
	d. Return on equity			
3.	Long-term solvency analysis			
	a. Debt to equity ratio			
	b. Interest coverage ratio			
4.	Cash flow adequacy analysis			
	a. Cash flow yield			
	b. Cash flows to sales			
	c. Cash flows to assets			
	d. Free cash flow			
5.	Market strength analysis			
	a. Price/earnings ratio			
	b. Dividends yield			

7.	Use of information from prior years

Name

Chapter 28, SE 1. Recording Sales: Fluctuating Exchange Rate

General Journal

Date	Description	Post. Ref.	Debit	Credit

Chapter 28, SE 2. Recording Purchases: Fluctuating Exchange Rate

Chapter 28, SE 3. Cost Adjusted to Market Method

Chapter 28, SE 4. Cost Adjusted to Market Method

Chapter 28, SE 5. Equity Method

General Journal

Date	Description	Post. Ref.	Debit	Credit

Chapter 28, SE 6. Methods of Accounting for Long-Term Investments

1.	
2.	
3.	

Chapter 28, SE 7. Purchase of 100 Percent at Book Value

Goodwill	
Minority Interest	
Common Stock	
Retained Earnings	

Chapter 28, SE 8. Purchase of Less than 100 Percent at Book Value

Goodwill	
Minority Interest	
Common Stock	
Retained Earnings	

Chapter 28, SE 9. Purchase of 100 Percent at More than Book Value

Goodwill	
Minority Interest	
Common Stock	
Retained Earnings	

Name

Chapter 28, SE 10. Intercompany Transactions

	T Company	C Company	Elimination	Consolidated
Accounts Receivable	230000 —	150000 —		
Accounts Payable	180000 —	90000 —		
Sales	1200000 —	890000 —		
Cost of Goods Sold	710000 —	540000 —		

Chapter 28, E 1. Recording International Transactions: Fluctuating Exchange

General Journal

Date	Description	Post. Ref.	Debit	Credit

Chapter 28, E 2. Recording International Transactions

General Journal

Date	Description	Post. Ref.	Debit	Credit

Chapter 28, E 3. Long-Term Investments

Date	Description	Post. Ref.	Debit	Credit

Name

Chapter 28, E 4. Long-Term Investments: Cost Adjusted to Market and Equity Methods

Chapter 28, E 5. Long-Term Investments: Equity Method

General Journal

Date	Description	Post. Ref.	Debit	Credit

Name

Chapter 28, E 6. Methods of Accounting for Long-Term Investments

1.

2.

3.

4.

5.

6.

Chapter 28, E 7. Elimination Entry for a Purchase at Book Value

General Journal

Date		Description	Post. Ref.	Debit	Credit

Chapter 28, E 8. Elimination Entry and Minority Interest

Name

Chapter 28, E 9. Consolidated Balance Sheet with Goodwill

Y and Z Companies
Work Sheet for Consolidated Balance Sheet
September 1, 20xx

Accounts	Balance Sheet, Y Company	Balance Sheet, Z Company	Eliminations Debit	Eliminations Credit	Consolidated Balance Sheet
Other Assets	2206000 —	1089000 —			
Investment in Z Company	960000 —				
Goodwill					
Total Assets	3166000 —	1089000 —			
Liabilities	871000 —	189000 —			
Common Stock, $1 par value	1000000 —	300000 —			
Retained Earnings	1295000 —	600000 —			
Total Liabilities and Stockholders' Equity	3166000 —	1089000 —			

Name ______________________

Chapter 28, E 10. Analyzing the Effects of Elimination Entries

A and B Companies
Work Sheet for Consolidated Balance Sheet
As of Acquisition Date

Accounts	Balance Sheet, A Company	Balance Sheet, B Company	Eliminations Debit	Eliminations Credit	Consolidated Balance Sheet
Accounts Receivable	260000—	80000—			
Interest Receivable, Bonds of B Company	1440—				
Investment in B Company	153000—				
Investment in B Company Bonds	36000—				
Accounts Payable	106000—	38000—			
Interest Payable, Bonds	6400—	4000—			
Bonds Payable	160000—	100000—			
Common Stock	200000—	120000—			
Retained Earnings	112000—	60000—			
Minority Interest					

Name ____________

Chapter 28, E 11. Preparation of Consolidated Income Statement

Polonia and Cardwell Companies
Work Sheet for Consolidated Income Statement
For the Year Ended December 31, 20x1

Accounts	Income Statement Polonia Company	Income Statement Cardwell Company	Eliminations Debit	Eliminations Credit	Consolidated Income Statement
Net Sales	3,000,000 —	1,200,000 —			
Cost of Goods Sold	1,500,000 —	800,000 —			
Gross Margin	1,500,000 —	400,000 —			
Less: Selling Expenses	500,000 —	100,000 —			
General and Administrative Expenses	600,000 —	200,000 —			
Total Operating Expenses	1,100,000 —	300,000 —			
Income from Operations	400,000 —	100,000 —			
Other Income	120,000 —	—			
Net Income	520,000 —	100,000 —			

Name ______________________

Chapter 28, P 1. International Transactions

General Journal

Date		Description	Post. Ref.	Debit	Credit

Name

General Journal

Date		Description	Post. Ref.	Debit	Credit

Name

General Journal				
Date	Description	Post. Ref.	Debit	Credit

Name

Chapter 28, P 2. Long-Term Investment Transactions

General Journal

Date	Description	Post. Ref.	Debit	Credit

Name ______________

General Journal

Date	Description	Post. Ref.	Debit	Credit

Name ____________________

Chapter 28, P 3. Long-Term Investments: Equity Method

1. Entries in journal form prepared

General Journal

Date	Description	Post. Ref.	Debit	Credit

Name

2. T account prepared

Investment in Sargent Company

Name ______________________

Chapter 28, P 4. Consolidated Balance Sheet: Less than 100 Percent Ownership

Kamper and Woolf Companies
Work Sheet for Consolidated Balance Sheet
As of Acquisition Date

Accounts	Balance Sheet, Kamper Company	Balance Sheet, Woolf Company	Eliminations Debit	Eliminations Credit	Consolidated Balance Sheet
Cash	320000—	48000—			
Accounts Receivable	520000—	240000—			
Inventory	800000—	520000—			
Investment in Woolf Company	593600—	—			
Property, Plant, and Equipment (net)	1200000—	880000—			
Other Assets	40000—	160000—			
Total Assets	3473600—	1848000—			
Accounts Payable	640000—	400000—			
Long-Term Debt	800000—	600000—			
Common Stock	1600000—	800000—			
Retained Earnings	433600—	48000—			
Minority Interest					
Total Liabilities and Stockholders' Equity	3473600—	1848000—			

Name

Chapter 28, P 5. Consolidated Balance Sheet: Cost Exceeding Book Value

Magreb and Nicario Companies
Work Sheet for Consolidated Balance Sheet
December 31, 20xx

Accounts	Balance Sheet, Magreb Company	Balance Sheet, Nicario Company	Eliminations Debit	Eliminations Credit	Consolidated Balance Sheet
Cash	120000 —	80000 —			
Accounts Receivable	200000 —	60000 —			
Investment in Nicario Company	700000 —	—			
Property, Plant, and Equipment	200000 —	360000 —			
Goodwill					
Total Assets	1220000 —	500000 —			
Accounts Payable	220000 —	60000 —			
Common Stock	800000 —	400000 —			
Retained Earnings	200000 —	40000 —			
Total Liabilities and Stockholders' Equity	1220000 —	500000 —			

Name

Chapter 28, P 6. Long-Term Investments Transactions

General Journal

Date	Description	Post. Ref.	Debit	Credit

Name

General Journal				
Date	Description	Post. Ref.	Debit	Credit

Name

Chapter 28, P 7. Long-Term Investments: Equity Method

1. Entries in journal form prepared

General Journal

Date		Description	Post. Ref.	Debit	Credit

Name

2. T account prepared

Investment in Albers Corporation

Name

Appendix A, P 1. Work Sheet, Financial Statements, and Closing Entries for a Merchandising Company: Periodic Inventory System

1. Work sheet completed (see page 439)
2. Income statement, statement of retained earnings, and balance sheet prepared

Metzler Music Store, Inc.
Income Statement
For the Year Ended November 30, 20x4

Net Sales			
Sales			306750 —

P 1 (continued)

Metzler Music Store, Inc.
Statement of Retained Earnings
For the Year Ended November 30, 20x4

Metzler Music Store, Inc.
Balance Sheet
November 30, 20x4

Assets

Liabilities

Stockholders' Equity

P 1 (concluded)

3. Closing entries prepared

General Journal

Date	Description	Post. Ref.	Debit	Credit

Name ______________________

Appendix A, P 2. Work Sheet, Financial Statements, and Closing Entries for a Merchandising Company: Periodic Inventory System

1. Work sheet prepared (see page 441)

2. Income statement, statement of retained earnings, and balance sheet prepared

Kirby Party Costumes Corporation				
Income Statement				
For the Year Ended June 30, 20x2				
Net Sales				475250 —

Name

P 2 (continued)

Kirby Party Costumes Corporation
Statement of Retained Earnings
For the Year Ended June 30, 20x2

Kirby Party Costumes Corporation
Balance Sheet
June 30, 20x2

Assets

Liabilities

Stockholders' Equity

Name

P 2 (concluded)

3. Closing entries prepared

General Journal

Date		Description	Post. Ref.	Debit	Credit

Name

Appendix B, P 1. Cash Receipts and Cash Payments Journals

1.	Transactions entered in cash receipts and cash payments journals
2.	Journals footed and crossfooted

Cash Receipts Journal — Page 1

			Debits			Credits		
Date	Account Debited/Credited	Post. Ref.	Cash	Sales Discounts	Other Accounts	Accounts Receivable	Sales	Other Accounts

Name ____________________

1, 2 (concluded)

Cash Payments Journal

Page 1

Date	Ck. No.	Payee	Account Credited/Debited	Post. Ref.	Credits: Cash	Credits: Purchases Discounts	Credits: Other Accounts	Debits: Accounts Payable	Debits: Other Accounts

Name

Appendix B, P 2. Purchases and General Journals

1. Transactions entered in general journal and purchases journal

General Journal — Page 1

Date		Description	Post. Ref.	Debit	Credit

Name ____________________

2. Purchases journal footed and crossfooted

					Purchases Journal							Page 1
					Credit	Debits						
										Other Accounts		
Date	Account Credited	Date of Invoice	Terms	Post. Ref.	Accounts Payable	Purchases	Freight In	Store Supplies	Office Supplies	Account	Post. Ref.	Amount

Name

3.	General ledger and accounts payable subsidiary ledger accounts opened and journals posted

General Ledger

Store Supplies — Account No. 116

Date		Post. Ref.	Debit	Credit	Balance Debit	Balance Credit

Office Supplies — Account No. 117

Date		Post. Ref.	Debit	Credit	Balance Debit	Balance Credit

Trucks — Account No. 142

Date		Post. Ref.	Debit	Credit	Balance Debit	Balance Credit

Office Equipment — Account No. 144

Date		Post. Ref.	Debit	Credit	Balance Debit	Balance Credit

Accounts Payable — Account No. 211

Date		Post. Ref.	Debit	Credit	Balance Debit	Balance Credit

3 (continued)

Purchases — Account No. 511

Date		Post. Ref.	Debit	Credit	Balance Debit	Balance Credit

Purchases Returns and Allowances — Account No. 512

Date		Post. Ref.	Debit	Credit	Balance Debit	Balance Credit

Freight In — Account No. 513

Date		Post. Ref.	Debit	Credit	Balance Debit	Balance Credit

Accounts Payable Subsidiary Ledger

Alvarez Company

Date		Post. Ref.	Debit	Credit	Balance

Daudridge Company

Date		Post. Ref.	Debit	Credit	Balance

Name ______________________

3 (concluded)

Hollins Company

Date		Post. Ref.	Debit	Credit	Balance

Meriweather Company

Date		Post. Ref.	Debit	Credit	Balance

Petrie Company

Date		Post. Ref.	Debit	Credit	Balance

Appendix B, P 3. Comprehensive Use of Special-Purpose Journals

1.	Special-purpose journals and general journal prepared
5.	Transactions entered in journals
6.	Journals footed and crossfooted

Sales Journal

Page 1

Date	Account Debited	Invoice Number	Terms	Post. Ref.	Amount (Debit/Credit Accounts Rec./Sales)

Name ______________________

Cash Receipts Journal								Page 1
			Debits			Credits		
Date	Account Debited/Credited	Post. Ref.	Cash	Sales Discounts	Other Accounts	Accounts Receivable	Sales	Other Accounts

Name ____________

Cash Payments Journal

Page 1

					Credits			Debits	
Date	Ck. No.	Payee	Account Credited/Debited	Post. Ref.	Cash	Purchases Discounts	Other Accounts	Accounts Payable	Other Accounts

Name

General Journal				Page 1
Date	Description	Post. Ref.	Debit	Credit

Name ____________________

2.	General ledger accounts opened
5.	Transactions posted
6.	End-of-month postings made

General Ledger

Cash — Account No. 111

Date		Post. Ref.	Debit	Credit	Balance Debit	Balance Credit

Accounts Receivable — Account No. 112

Date		Post. Ref.	Debit	Credit	Balance Debit	Balance Credit

Office Equipment — Account No. 141

Date		Post. Ref.	Debit	Credit	Balance Debit	Balance Credit

Accounts Payable — Account No. 211

Date		Post. Ref.	Debit	Credit	Balance Debit	Balance Credit

Name

2, 5, 6 (continued)

Sales — Account No. 411

Date		Post. Ref.	Debit	Credit	Balance Debit	Balance Credit

Sales Discounts — Account No. 412

Date		Post. Ref.	Debit	Credit	Balance Debit	Balance Credit

Sales Returns and Allowanaces — Account No. 413

Date		Post. Ref.	Debit	Credit	Balance Debit	Balance Credit

Purchases — Account No. 511

Date		Post. Ref.	Debit	Credit	Balance Debit	Balance Credit

Purchases Discounts — Account No. 512

Date		Post. Ref.	Debit	Credit	Balance Debit	Balance Credit

Purchases Returns and Allowances — Account No. 513

Date		Post. Ref.	Debit	Credit	Balance Debit	Balance Credit

2, 5, 6 (concluded)

Freight In — Account No. 514

Date		Post. Ref.	Debit	Credit	Balance Debit	Balance Credit

Sales Salaries Expense — Account No. 521

Date		Post. Ref.	Debit	Credit	Balance Debit	Balance Credit

Advertising Expense — Account No. 522

Date		Post. Ref.	Debit	Credit	Balance Debit	Balance Credit

Rent Expense — Account No. 531

Date		Post. Ref.	Debit	Credit	Balance Debit	Balance Credit

Repairs Expense — Account No. 532

Date		Post. Ref.	Debit	Credit	Balance Debit	Balance Credit

Name

3.	Accounts receivable subsidiary ledger accounts opened
5.	Transactions posted

Accounts Receivable Subsidiary Ledger

C. Jambois

Date			Post. Ref.	Debit	Credit	Balance

B. Kahn

Date			Post. Ref.	Debit	Credit	Balance

L. Nomura

Date			Post. Ref.	Debit	Credit	Balance

Name

4.	Accounts payable subsidiary ledger accounts opened
5.	Transactions posted

Accounts Payable Subsidiary Ledger

Chacon Company

Date			Post. Ref.	Debit	Credit	Balance

Keagy Company

Date			Post. Ref.	Debit	Credit	Balance

Passarelli Manufacturing

Date			Post. Ref.	Debit	Credit	Balance

WMBT

Date			Post. Ref.	Debit	Credit	Balance

Name

7. Trial balance and schedules of accounts receivable and payable prepared

Sanchez Refrigeration Company
Trial Balance
October 31, 20xx

Sanchez Refrigeration Company
Schedule of Accounts Receivable
October 31, 20xx

Sanchez Refrigeration Company
Schedule of Accounts Payable
October 31, 20xx

Name

Appendix C, P 1. Partnership Formation and Distribution of Income

1.	Journal entry prepared

2.	Share of income for each partner determined
a.	Income shared equally

	20x1	20x2

b.	No agreement
c.	Income shared on the basis of the partners' original investments

	20x1	20x2

Name

d.	Interest on investment; remainder shared equally			
	20x1 computation:	Income of Partner		Income
		Himes	Palmer	Distributed

	20x2 computation:	Income of Partner		Income
		Himes	Palmer	Distributed

Name

e.	Salaries allowed; remainder shared equally			
	20x1 computation:	**Income of Partner**		**Income**
		Himes	**Palmer**	**Distributed**

	20x2 computation:	**Income of Partner**		**Income**
		Himes	**Palmer**	**Distributed**

Name

f.	Interest and salaries allowed; remainder shared equally			
	20x1 computation:	Income of Partner		Income
		Himes	Palmer	Distributed

	20x2 computation:	Income of Partner		Income
		Himes	Palmer	Distributed

Name

Appendix C, P 2. Admission and Withdrawal of a Partner

	General Journal				
	Date	Description	Post. Ref.	Debit	Credit
a.					
b.					
c.					

Computation:

Name

Partners' capital ratios:

General Journal

Date		Description	Post. Ref.	Debit	Credit
d.					

Computation:

Name

	Date		Description	Post. Ref.	Debit	Credit
			General Journal			
e.						

Computation:

	Date		Description	Post. Ref.	Debit	Credit
f.						

Name

Appendix D, E 1. Future Value Calculations

(1) Simple interest

(2) Compounded semiannually

(3) Compounded quarterly

(4) Compounded monthly

Appendix D, E 2. Future Value Calculations

(1) Single payment of $20,000 at 7% for 10 years

(2) Ten annual payments of $2,000 at 7%

(3) Single payment of $6,000 at 9% for 7 years

(4) Seven annual payments of $6,000 at 9%

Name

Appendix D, E 3. Future Value Calculations

(1) Compounded annually

(2) Compounded semiannually

(3) Compounded quarterly

Appendix D, E 4. Future Value Calculations

(1) 10% compounded annually

(2) 10% compounded semiannually

Year	Balance	x	Rate	=	Interest	Deposits

Name

2 (continued)

Optional: Alternative Solution

(3) 4% compounded annually

Name ______________________

E 4 (concluded)

(4)	16% compounded quarterly					
Year	**Balance**		**Rate**		**Interest**	**Deposits**
1		x		=		
1		x		=		
1		x		=		
1		x		=		
2		x		=		
2		x		=		
2		x		=		
2		x		=		
3		x		=		
3		x		=		
3		x		=		
3		x		=		
4		x		=		
4		x		=		
4		x		=		
4		x		=		
End of						
year 4						

Optional: Alternative Solution

Form is not provided; student should use his/her own paper.

Name

Appendix D, E 5. Future Value Applications

a. Required rate of return, $20,000 invested, $40,000 needed in 12 years

b. Time required for $40,000 at 7% to accumulate to $64,000

Appendix D, E 6. Working Backward from a Future Value

Appendix D, E 7. Determining an Advance Payment

Appendix D, E 8. Present Value Calculations

(1) Single payment of $24,000 at 6% for 12 years

(2) Annual payments of $2,000 at 6% for 12 years

(3) Single payment of $5,000 at 9% for 5 years

(4) Five annual payments of $5,000 at 9%

Name ______________________

Appendix D, E 9. Present Value of a Lump-Sum Contract

	Years	Rate	Factor	Present Value of $60,000
(1)				
(2)				
(3)				
(4)				

Appendix D, E 10. Present Value of an Annuity Contract

	Pay- ments	Rate	Factor	Present Value of $1,200 Payments
(1)				
(2)				
(3)				
(4)				

Name

Appendix D, E 11. Non-Interest-Bearing Note

Computations:

Name

E 11 (concluded)

1. To record purchase on Pendleton records and sale on Leyland records

General Journal

Date	Description	Post. Ref.	Debit	Credit
	Pendleton Journal			
	Leyland Journal			

2. To adjust interest expense and interest income at the end of first year

Date	Description	Post. Ref.	Debit	Credit
	Pendleton Journal			
	Leyland Journal			

3. To record interest expense and interest income and payment of the note at the end of the second year

Date	Description	Post. Ref.	Debit	Credit
	Pendleton Journal			
	Leyland Journal			

Appendix D, E 12. Valuing an Asset for the Purpose of Making a Purchasing Decision

Appendix D, E 13. Deferred Payment

Journal entries prepared:

General Journal

Date	Description	Post. Ref.	Debit	Credit

Name

E 13 (concluded)

General Journal

Date		Description	Post. Ref.	Debit	Credit

Appendix D, E 14. Investment of Idle Cash

Journal entries prepared:

Name

Appendix D, E 15. Accumulation of a Fund

Appendix D, E 16. Negotiating the Sale of a Business

Raftson's offer to sell:

From Table 4 in the appendix on future value and present value tables:

Ruiz's offer to buy:

From Table 4 in the appendix on future value and present value tables: